# TO HEAR A GIRL SCREAM

Thank you!

♡ common

Cobb

# TO HEAR
# A GIRL
# SCREAM

## A MEMOIR OF DREAMS AND
## INSIGHTS IN THE 21ST CENTURY

## CAMRYN COBB

NEW DEGREE PRESS

TO HEAR A GIRL SCREAM

*A Memoir of Dreams and Insights in the 21st Century*

ISBN    978-1-64137-918-2  *Paperback*

            978-1-64137-683-9  *Kindle Ebook*

            978-1-64137-685-3  *Ebook*

To my selfless and strong-willed parents.
Mama and Daddy...
This book is the result of a lifetime of allowing me to think for myself
and providing me the resources to do so. I am nothing without you.

And to my hometown and city of Brunswick, Georgia...
Thank you for challenging me, pushing me, and
making me want to run away.
Rest in Peace, Ahmaud Arbery. I still run for you.

# Table of Contents

**PART FOUR**

*"Until we can all present ourselves to the world in our completeness, as fully and beautifully as we see ourselves naked in our bedrooms, we are not free."*

# Author's Note

*Angry black girl.* I was twenty years old before someone finally told me what it was. I constantly wondered, *why can't they hear me?* Why does it feel like the world stops listening to me the moment I begin to speak? Why does it feel like I am constantly screaming underwater?

So, I would think, *maybe I should talk louder!* Use words that hold more Power when I respond to insensitive comments. Evoke emotion through my body language if they dare to converse with me. Refrain from blinking or revealing any jitters when they avoid eye contact with me. Force them to feel me, which, in return, just might force them to hear me.

I would morph my opinions into something reactionary, and while I was being bold, I unknowingly forced myself into a mold created for me. Little did I know, my Powerful expression took everything away from the words I spoke. Ya know, it was my Powerful expression in conjunction with my blackness and my womanhood. We all know that black people are always complaining, and women are inevitably upset. That is why I was seen as the angry black girl and why no one would ever hear me.

The world has likely been suggesting that I reframe my opinion with special safe words that wouldn't be offensive to the receiver—who would likely be a lot different from me and would probably disagree with me. In many ways, I think that is complete nonsense. But the message that it was time to change my approach was loud, clear, and forever helpful to me. I cannot change the way people view me or interpret my words, but I can commit to my stance and refuse to question the validity of my own experiences. As the sender of the message, I must show that I will never be ashamed to be the angry black girl and will always demand to be heard.

Women of color all over the world lose their voice every time someone perpetuates this idea that their tone or passion keeps them from deserving to be heard. It doesn't matter if it is a woman of color at home, in the workplace, or in the White House—someone or multiple someones will always act like they are completely tone-deaf to the message because they assume they already know what will be said. It doesn't matter if these women of color were actually treated unfairly, forced into an oppressive situation, or had every reason in the world to be angry. The world will assume they already know their story, and that they are oh-so-tired of that same broken record. And for all of those same reasons, these twenty-first-century women are still fetishized, denied care, imprisoned, abused, and silenced.

Believe it or not, the words we use and the ways we think don't just live in our heads and in our homes. Unfortunately, life isn't a video game or a Lifetime movie. The ideas we cultivate in our minds are spewed out into the world around us whether they are good, bad, or ugly.

These kinds of social constructions, stereotypes, and ideas keep us from connecting and coexisting with one another. It isn't because some of us are black or white, male or female, legal or illegal. It isn't because we choose to vote red or blue or are economically fiscal or socially liberal. It isn't because some of us are religious and others aren't. It's not even that some of us were born into wealth and others weren't as lucky. None of these things divide us. The problems start in how we communicate with each other and the giant invisible, sometimes physical, walls that we build up to separate ourselves from each other... creating so much chaos and commotion that we can't even hear each other.

* * *

After spending years battling myself about who I was and what I stood for, as a biracial female raised in the formerly Confederate Georgia, I have finally found a way to confidently scream from the rooftops. I know now that I will never make a change by proving I am right or that someone else is wrong. I can let the anger in my heart explode out of me, but I am also allowed to cry and express pain. I can facilitate conversation and come to agreements, but I can also disagree completely if I want to. I know now I can be both black and a woman while also demanding to be heard in ways far greater than my initial reaction, even in ways that could be considered revolutionary.

Though I am still young, I can dream of a more supportive environment that would make both the indigenous people of our land and the founding fathers of our country proud of what the United States of America has become. I am doing this even before reaching the legal drinking age or being old enough to vote in a presidential election cycle because I want to share my experiences. I am covered in and created by experiences that allow me to interact with others unlike me and exist in a world that creates so much dissonance.

I created this book by allowing myself to be completely vulnerable, open-minded, and true to myself and my identity—searching for answers and explanations that could potentially help me make sense of the world around me. So this is my story. These are anecdotes that make me a human just like you. They outline my different lived experiences in the past twenty years... from the times I felt overjoyed, accomplished, or lucky to the times I felt humiliated, confused, or even stupid. Overall, this is the story of learning to use my voice while existing in a world where I am constantly being silenced.

With this book, I want to connect with my peers by sharing my own stories, experiences, and sometimes outlandish thoughts. I believe my cohort, Generation Z, was privileged enough to be born into a technological era, but unfortunately, we were still gifted many of the consequences of generations before us—a dysfunctional government, segregated social structures, learned hatred and oppression, a depleted environment, and the list goes on.

I am speaking to and for the young people who, like me, want to take a stab at saving the world. Together, we will explore what that might look like and how our past experiences could drive this rescue of the universe. While I am often talking directly to my youthful counterparts, I encourage all open-minded and wise souls to join us in the exploration of what the future could and will be—allowing ourselves to navigate new possibilities we were never exposed to, assuring ourselves that we can be critical of our learned habits and ways of thinking while recognizing the lessons and wisdom to be extracted from the past.

It is time that I finally connect beyond a cryptic tweet or passive post, through real words that hold real weight, while still allowing the reader enough space and consent to create their own thoughts and opinions. I want my peers to read more than 140 characters at a time because longer works have the context and nuance that no tweet can muster.

Our Facebook feeds and Twitter timelines swarm with words full of animosity and responses reeking of undeniable tension. As young people existing in this polarized and robotic setting, we cannot waste any more time. We will not fight to make older generations validate our lived experiences. We will not try to convince them to vote in favor of our opinions. We will not feel hopeless when our elected representatives don't act in favor of our needs.

Instead, we will become the generation to not only unapologetically share our experiences but decide to actually listen to each other's differing stories. We will not only show up to vote ourselves, but we will ensure that each of us can utilize that right. We will stop relying on the people in charge who don't represent us and become people who work as fearless leaders for those who cannot speak for themselves. We will do this for all the humans and creatures inhabiting our country currently and for all the souls who will explore this land in years to come. Our fight is not to make our country great again but to make our country, at the very least, comfortable, sustainable, and habitable.

It is not about the years we spend on this green earth but about the multitude of adventures, encounters, and hardships we face. My experiences and your experiences are painted by the effects of what we have encountered together as citizens in this country. Each of these experiences gives the people more Power. Politics are personal, and, because of that, we are being called to join the same movement—not a movement that forces us to pick one ideology over the other but a movement wherein we find our humanity again and rediscover the things that make us all equal members of one human family.

Telling our stories won't cure all the issues of today, but it could surely jumpstart the movement tailored just for us. Once we allow ourselves to discover the depth of each other's souls and the legitimacy of each other's realities, we will join hand in hand to create the rules and policies that will allow each of us to grow and flourish into something independently Powerful.

If we use our innovative minds to mobilize such a movement inside the billion-dollar walls of our unchanging country, maybe the young, wide-eyed people who come after us could actually change the entire world—a world where we would all have warm beds and full tummies.

Thank you for listening to me dream. And thank you for hearing me scream.

# PART ONE

# The Year 1999

It was the year 1999. I was born on a military base in Georgia just two hours shy of April Fool's day, making my very first comedic entrance. I was an infant in 1999, so I don't remember much about that year. But those who were adults at the time had experiences just like mine.

The last year of the '90s. The last year in the thousands of years that started with 1. The number 99 is tattooed in Old English on my ankle and resented by my mother. After a short twenty years, even the year 1999 has secrets to uncover.

They say history repeats itself, and we all know it's true. The decades go by. We live and we die. But over time... does the world not learn to love a little more or to fight a little less? How has the world not learned how to make any sense of its own mess?

Let's party like it's 1999. Prince said it best. It sounds revitalizing... out of context. Even though this song was released over a decade before the year 1999, this invitation to the world to party encapsulates the sad reality of that year. He wasn't just calling for a party. He speaks of war and bombs. He embraces the fact that life could be cut short at any second. These words spilled out of his mouth and onto dance floors during the night.

But I imagine everyone just continued to dance. It makes me wonder. Did anything hold enough weight to stop the party? Or turn it around? Or make someone at least turn the music down?

But I imagine it felt good to just keep dancing—dancing for the things to live for.

This was the year that SpongeBob premiered.[1] My childhood and so many others would change forever. Myspace was introduced to the internet.[2] It was the first relevant social media website, and it wasn't Facebook. Apple released the iBook, which would be considered the first "affordable" portable computer.[3] Google moved out of a garage and into an actual workspace, just one step closer to becoming one of the largest companies in the world in the coming years.[4]

Little did the world know, these things were the exact reason why children like me would stop playing outside in the years to come. Technology would creep in and reveal itself slowly over the next few years. I'd become less connected to the humans around me and more connected with the virtual

---

1   "What Happened In 1999 Pop Culture, Prices and Events," The People History, accessed April 14, 2020.

2   Ibid.

3   Ibid.

4   Ibid.

versions of my peers. More time on Nintendos and less time in the sun, our screens illuminated our faces as we searched for more fun.

It wasn't just the influx of technology though. Riots, shootings, and corruption kept rocking the world. But there was no time for despair. So everyone kept dancing. There's always time for at least one more twirl.

It was the year 1999, just eighteen days after I was born. Two teen boys walked into a school in Littleton, Colorado. They replaced their regular school supplies with guns and bombs—strapped with revenge and their second amendment right, filled with angst and teenage-boy might. At seventeen and eighteen, they became murderers. They took the lives of others and, as a grand finale, killed themselves. It was the deadliest mass shooting—twenty injured and thirteen pronounced dead. The Columbine High School massacre, that's what the news said.[5]

The news spoke of something that gut-wrenching for the very first time. Little did they know, they'd be reporting that same horrific event repeatedly over time. The kindness of our human hearts and the reality of the broken world don't always align.

I imagine everyone just continued to dance. To the rhythm of Prince speaking of war. I wonder if the US government was setting an example of violence, hate, weapons—always

5    History.com Editors, "Columbine Shooting," HISTORY, 2009, accessed
     April 14, 2020.

asking for more. These things showed up in our schools, and somehow everyone still chose to ignore.

Over the next twenty years, I learned the alphabet, simple trigonometry, how to hold conversations, and how to live without my mommy. Yet the people who hold the most Power in my country still have not learned that it's time to protect— to save their students in the classroom—not time to neglect.

At Sandy Hook Elementary School, twenty first-graders were shot dead.[6] At Marjory Stoneman Douglas High School, seventeen were murdered with bright futures ahead.[7] The perpetrators? Always fueled by trauma and the sick thoughts in their head. Is school an environment for learning or does it act as a battlefield set for micro-aggressions to come alive instead?

But they just keep dancing to the music, blaring the sound so loud that it becomes therapeutic.

It was the year 1999. Bill Clinton was acquitted. The United States Senate declared indulging in infidelity did not make you an unfit president.[8] Now I know that not much will. But did anyone consider Monica Lewinsky, a young woman interning in the White House? I suppose she is considered a homewrecker or a whore. But how was she not protected

---

6   History.com Editors, "Sandy Hook School Shooting," HISTORY, 2013, accessed April 14, 2020.

7   History.com Editors, "Teen Gunman Kills 17, Injures 17 At Parkland, Florida High School," HISTORY, 2019, accessed April 14, 2020.

8   "What Happened In 1999 Pop Culture, Prices and Events."

from being exposed to the President of the United States? Where is this argument in the debates?

Over the next twenty years, we referenced this time in history. But President Clinton's wife, Hillary, was in the hot seat this time. A woman was the closest she had ever been to smashing the patriarchy and receiving the highest position of Power in the land. But they would say, "How could she be president if she couldn't even get her husband to commit?" And magically, just like that, this same situation was finally enough to make someone unfit.

We live in a man's world. This has always been true. Girls wear pink, and boys wear blue. And the male must always hold the most Power of the two.

Whether it was an affair with the president or a nomination to be the president, Monica and Hillary never received any empathy. As women, they are forced to wear their sins like badges. Socially constructed to move with grace, they should just do what they know best—shut up and move on. They should refrain from having a voice or anything that would potentially remove a man from his throne.

The music stopped a long time ago, but people keep dancing. Tragedy is all around us, but we just keep prancing.

Twenty years have gone by, and everything is the same. I don't see any less hatred or any less pain. How did we forget to embrace any change? I find the refusal to grow so strange. We find the time to converse about these things on our timelines, but we allow the important conversations to patiently wait on the sidelines.

Looking back in time, we find the blueprint of today's world. Just throw in a million more computers and other forms of technology, and there you have it—the very beginning of what would become the era of the 2000s, much different from all the eras before. Somehow the benefits of our technological world are nearly unrecognizable. As the days go by and the world stays the same, we become more liable.

I want the present day to look different than it did in 1999. It's time for our values and goals to be redefined.

# Saving the World and Self

Today I am twenty years old. I'll never be younger than this moment. I have the most energy and the least amount of wrinkles. I am so full of emotions, compassion, thoughts, and ideas. If these things were fuel, I'm certain I could power a car across the whole nation.

The beautiful moments sneak their way in—the moments where we love, share, care, connect, depend, and feel all of the things within. They say the rain makes the rainbow. It's the pain makes the world grow.

Yet I feel so tired, so defeated, as if I lost a battle that I haven't even fought—a battle I pulled up late to, as if I only caught the end of it. And unfortunately, the ending is terrible. So now I am so full of passion and pain that I am almost sure I could change the entire world.

Many people don't "involve" themselves with politics or anything of the sort. The heavy, confusing stuff that usually comes with some sort of hurt, the reality of our interactions, the way we govern and organize our human community. We all have this in common, and no one can be granted immunity.

Some of us choose to participate because, to us, there is no choice. The policy decisions being made directly affect us and those around us. It is a privilege to choose to not be involved, to assume the world's problems have already been solved.

Whenever people ask what I'm interested in, the first thing that comes to my mind is politics. I usually get a wide-eyed facial expression and a reply that confirms many people hate the subject.

Our constitution reads "We the People." We are the individuals behind the People who have the Power. Someone must take the job and involve themselves. Many young people feel like it is now being left to us. By us, I mean Generation Z, or the people around my age group, or whoever we claim to be—the young people, the college students, the Instagram influencers, and everyone in-between.

But why talk about politics when Yeezy dropped new shoes on his website a few days ago? Why talk about politics when pretty girls are dancing in every Instagram video? When you're one click away from the newest fashion trend? One click away from the next viral video? One click away from your next boyfriend?

Just one click away from turning your bad day into a good day. One click away from the smiles, laughs, congratulations, celebrations, and conglomerations. One click away from the births, deaths, conversations, confrontations, and complications.

Many of our thoughts are guided by the devices in front of us. You see, that is the thing about being just one click away. You have a smartphone in hand or a computer nearby. You have a watch on your wrist or iPad in your bag. It is always there, but it isn't always fair. You feel bombarded by new content yet can't pull yourself away. Sometimes you will scroll upon the most revitalizing content. Sometimes you will come upon something that really sets fire up your ass—something you wish you had never seen or something you wish would just go away.

For me, political posts often light a fire in my soul.

What makes me love politics as much as I hate it? Is it the fact that talking about it can make my heart beat fast and my blood boil? Or how sometimes I leave a conversation feeling like I may understand the world a little bit more? I think it's because politics is personal. It is everywhere, and it affects everyone. In my mind, it is the root of all good and evil. So if you're looking to save the world... it's easy to fall into.

I believe we all face the same questions: Will you save the world or yourself? Do you want to go on fancy vacations and drive nice cars? Meet fancy people and be invited to nice bars? Is it enough to pay the bills and feed your children? Or do you dream of giving back to the community and affecting people by the millions?

I think most people want it all. We want the nice things we feel we deserve. We want happy families and good memories. We want to feel needed and important. We want to feel supported and rewarded. But we also want to share these feelings with the rest of the world. We want each man to be granted the "pursuit of happiness," as the constitution promised.

I made my decision at a very young age. In elementary school, I wanted to be a judge, lawyer, or professor—someone who had the Power to do something, to do everything. I wasn't sure. I just knew things were wrong and people needed help.

My extended family had different lives than I did. Some lived in trailer parks. Others lived in the projects. Some lived just across town, but none of them had the same opportunities I did. I watched my relatives rely on food stamps and Section 8 while my Christmases were filled with every gift I could ever want.

My parents had friends who were incarcerated from time to time. We would go put money on their books. My parents had friends who couldn't keep a job, but for their kids, they would lie, kill, and rob. My parents had friends who struggled with addiction and some who fed others' addictions to put food on the table. This didn't make me or my family any better. This allowed us to be thankful for having a stable life.

My mother ingrained in me the value of supporting and forgiving others. She did anything she could to help those in need, without judgment. She taught me that no matter what life brings, we are all just humans at our core. Others' issues are our issues, and these are things we cannot ignore.

So for me, answering the question was easy. Did I want to save the world or save myself? As the daughter of a woman who works in the finance department for a Chapter 13 bankruptcy trustee and a man who dedicated twenty-four years of his life to the U.S. Navy, I wanted to do both. As the daughter of a white woman and a black man who grew up in the South and had mixed babies in the '90s, I wanted to do both. As the descendant of poor white farm people and African slaves, I really just wanted to do both.

I wanted to save the world and save myself.

# Generation Zoomer

Millennial. Gen X. Baby Boomer. Cohorts of the past. It's now time to make way for Generation Zoomer—Generation Z, officially. We are an entire generation of dreamers. Our time on Earth was long-awaited.

Born from 1997 to 2012, we are the last of the '90s babies to the beginning babies of something new.

Facebook would say we are lazy. Twitter would suggest our back-up jobs should be in comedy. LinkedIn would confirm that we will likely change jobs frequently. Zooming away from the things that don't serve us. Zooming toward things that make us feel some sort of purpose.

We are described as "tech-savvy, politically involved, realistic, and globally engaged."[9] We are a mix of races and ethnicities. We run the spectrum of sexuality. We refuse gender roles and toxic social constructions. We subscribe

---

9   Sam Tetrault, "What Is a Zoomer (Gen Z) & Who's Considered One?" Cake Blog, 2020, accessed April 17, 2020.

to acceptance and freedom. We unsubscribe from hatred and bigotry. We are eclectic souls who make creating peace our responsibility.

The oldest of our generation watched the Twin Towers fall; witnessed the war in Afghanistan; endured a recession; were gifted a divided, broken country as we entered adulthood— hanging on to hope as we move forward, dreaming of the truly free land our constitution ordered.

Many of us grew up on the internet; prematurely exposed to the greatest and worst content we could find; introduced to things that would help us define our identities; acquainted with drama, turmoil, and obscenities.

We grew up together, all of us around the world. No matter how far apart, we experienced our lives with the eyes of the world watching, which came with tying our worth to likes and followers. We were drenched in the pressure to be like everyone else while also feeling like we should stand out. Troubled by the consequences of social media, we could not deny the opportunity to constantly connect. Granted platforms to share our stories and profiles to share our worries.

Pushing the envelope away from what is expected. Miles from what is considered traditional. Light years away from what is shoved down our throats. Demanded in our homes. And reinforced in our schools.

We zoom from here to there. We zoom everywhere. We fill up the hip-hop, rap, and EDM concerts. We fill the college campuses. We fill the entry-level jobs. We are the most diverse demographic, soon to become the most educated generation.[10]

We are prepared to do the necessary work to make America a greater nation.

---

10   Hansi Lo Wang, "Generation Z Is the Most Racially and Ethnically Diverse Yet," NPR, 2018, accessed April 17, 2020.

# The Purple House

I wonder all the time whether it's enough to vote during an
election cycle while worrying about the state of our country and our futures in the meantime. I wonder if everyone
around me wonders too or if I'm just overly sensitive, dramatic, and responsible for painting my own world blue.

A little blue dot in a big red sea. Although, I'm not sure the
blue dot even represents me. Sometimes I want to be purple.
Picking a side feels like choosing between strep or the flu. But
deciding to be in the middle feels like I am still complying
with the idea of the two.

Deep down, I know my vote simply isn't enough. And I am
not sure it ever will be—not when the people who supposedly
represent us don't even look like you or me. We don't talk
the same or dress the same or even act like we are from the
same century.

Why don't we the People ever get to be the leaders of our own
world? When I speak of them, in opposition to us, I speak

of many. They fill up the *White* House, which I think they meant quite literally.

Little girls like me who dream of making a change deserve to see faces that look like theirs in Congress. Brown faces. Girl faces. Angry faces. Emotional faces. Gay faces. Overly passionate faces. Faces willing to let loose because they are aware of how their policy decisions affect us. Faces that won't just speak for those who are silenced but are willing to go above and beyond to protect us.

What if we become the people who regulate our livelihood? The ones who control the funding? The ones in charge of our safety? No dream candidate will magically appear and make our country a better place. We are the dream candidates who need to join the race.

To those who can articulate their thoughts, we need you to be our speakers. To those who have a way with words, we need you to be our writers. To those who can teach others, we need you to be our educators. To those who can think out of the box, we need you to be our strategists. Together, we will create an entire generation that resists.

We can reject the cruel parts of the world that don't serve us, the politicians who don't represent us, the systems that hurt us. We can create a world that is actually *for* us.

But first, we must purge the parts of ourselves that think we can't. The voices in our heads that tell us we aren't smart enough, strong enough, and don't have enough money or resources. We must silence those voices and get to work. We are the People. We are what keeps things going— the ulti-mate force behind the system. We must reject the idea that we are the victims.

As W.E.B. Dubois said, "A system cannot fail those who it was never meant to protect."

In this new world, there will be no victims. If we refuse to accept anything they feed to us, we will eventually become self-sufficient—no longer held back by the way we were conditioned.

So what if we march in together? This time we won't waste our energy by sitting across from them and sharing our sad stories, hoping that maybe they can emphasize with us. We have no more time to cry and lobby, no more time to wish for the change we want to see—only time to do everything necessary to proceed.

It's time we wake up without the feeling of hopelessness. We will get dressed in our very worn clothes with rips and holes. We will use our calloused hands to gather our materials, and we will use our aching feet to march to the White House. This two-hundred-year-old home needs renovating. Let's paint it in shades of purple, lavender, orchid, lilac. Let's replace everything outdated and old.

The house will no longer be White and calm—it will be col-orful, noisy, and bold.

# PART TWO

# Daddy's Little Girl

Daddy, I know I always speak of how men often disgust me. I go on and on for hours about how their toxic masculinity and selfishness revolts me. But I hope you know that I will always be your little girl. You are the man who built my entire world.

You have always seen the greatness within me and made sure I had the life where I could be whoever I wanted to be. Unlike the selfish men I speak of, you committed your life to my brother and me by serving in the military to make sure we grew up in a stable home, giving both necessities and the freedom to roam.

We never had to grow up in projects or dangerous neighborhoods. We never had to work throughout high school to buy our own school clothes or eat ramen noodles for most of our dinners. You gave us everything we needed and still let us accomplish things on our own because we were just winners.

But you didn't just make sure we were fed and clothed; you made us black. Your genes gave us a culture I didn't even realize I had. Way greater than just the love of rap music and basketball, you gave us the part of our identity that makes our hair grow into afros, grants us black excellence, and makes our personalities more intriguing to everyone we interact with. Some would probably say the combination of your blackness and my mother's white skin has made our lives harder, but I would say it makes me fight harder.

You are the black man that all my white family expected to fail us, but you always proved them wrong by never raising your voice and only ever loving us. You built the foundation that has allowed me to go to college and continue to be loud. You never question anything I do, and you are always proud.

I could never thank you enough for being a father I can lean on. You never had one of those, but you became the man you didn't have a blueprint for. That's how I know I can be anything I want to be. I can be the first in our family to go to college. I can be a black woman who becomes a senator one day. I don't need to rely on anyone else to pave the way.

You were deployed for years out of my life but somehow found the time to take me on movie dates and sometimes tried to do my hair. You took me to black barbershops with you and became the reason I love Usher and Kanye. You are the first and only man who will always love me. You taught me to always be my own person and never succumb to the things expected of me.

You are the reason behind my existence. You are the reason I radiate black brilliance. You are the reason for the brown skin I cherish so much. You are the reason behind my big hair and every little curl. That is why I will always be daddy's little girl.

# A Letter to My Mama

Mama, I never feel anger toward you. Sometimes my words slip out and become charged with intensity, each of them carefully packaged with an immense amount of density.

But the thought of you could bring me to tears. You have enough strength built up inside of you that it has carried us both through life. In fact, it is so powerful that it has carried our entire family through each of our lives. I am not sure if they know, but I do. Mama, I know. Your sacrifices ride with me too.

It's so beautiful that you never speak a word of the pain you encountered in the past. You only speak of praises and blessings. You only think of the next people you can help. You only find new ways to build yourself up just enough to act as someone to lean on—knowing that when you lean, you can only fall. So you always decide you will only stand tall.

You don't always understand why I speak so often of the pain that paints the road we and others walk on. Mama, I know you only want things for me you never had for you—security, ease, freedom from burden. But you don't know that you have already given me these things. You have taught me to never let them be taken away. That's why when I speak, I use words that weigh.

You didn't always understand that it is my duty to always fight against those holding people in my community underwater, to speak up and speak loud. Because when I look at my skin, I am proud.

You didn't always know that you are the one who started my revolution, the movement inside my heart. You loved a black man and didn't care who disapproved. Mama, you are the reason I wake up every day and feel moved.

They say you learn about self-image from your mother. She teaches you how to do your makeup and how to fix your hair. But your skin never looked like mine, and my hair was thick while yours was fine.

I didn't always know that you and I were not the same. You were once just the woman who birthed me, raised me, did my hair, fed me, disciplined me, clothed me, and provided me care—my superwoman, the protagonist in all my biggest dreams, the last face I saw at night and the first to wake me up in the morning. I didn't always know we were not the same. I didn't always know the nature of the race game.

I didn't know about the game where the color of my father's black skin caused shame, where isolation from others caused my white mother's pain. I didn't always know that family meant following the status quo, doing what you're told, sticking to your own, never disrupting the flow.

But you and I know that my thick country accent kinda sounds like yours. And when people look in my eyes, all they see is a reflection of you. We know that you gave me my intensity, my willpower, my loud mouth, and my brainpower.

And because of you and my very black father, I have all the tools I need to fight against the system. Don't ask why. Don't ask how. All I need you to do is listen.

Mama, I am glad you and I are not the same. You gave me all of your privilege and made a generational change. You are a white woman, but you birthed brown children. You provided me with armor. And when they see me, they will know that can never disarm her.

# Mixed with Two

I didn't always know my mom and I were not the same. She never pointed out our different shades of skin, and she was not to blame. For God's sake, in Pre-K, I wanted Tim McGraw's picture on my birthday cake. I had no idea I was supposed to be all mixed and confused like Drake.

I blame all the institutions, stereotypes, and defaults for making me stand on the playground in kindergarten and wonder where to play. With those kids or those kids? What will be okay?

I don't look like her, and I don't look like him. I look a little different from all of them.

I blame my second-grade teacher for using me to teach the new generation about Martin Luther King Jr. I guess no one told her not to call out the one biracial kid to use as an example. She boldly exclaimed, "If it weren't for Martin Luther King, people like Camryn's parents couldn't be together."

She failed to mention that people like her white parents would potentially hate people like my parents but only discreetly. She failed to mention it took until the year before Martin Luther King's assassination and the supreme court case, Loving v. Virginia, for people of different races to love freely.[11]

It wasn't until 1967, only a few years before the birth of my parents, that Chief Justice Earl Warren concluded, "The freedom to marry, or not marry, a person of another race resides with the individual and cannot be infringed by the State."[12] No wonder my parents' union felt illegal to my grandparents and others. I cannot blame them for being products of their culture. I blame systematic racism and its rigid structure.

My second-grade teacher also failed to mention that neither Martin Luther King Jr. nor the Supreme Court case could change a prejudiced person's mind, and they would always just think that way. I didn't volunteer to be the poster child for interracial marriage, but I remained that way for the next decade. The consequences of the exposé of my racial identity started as quickly as that day.

By that day, I mean seconds later, seconds after we learned who Martin Luther King Jr. was and I learned that my parents were different than everyone else's—as if that wasn't a hard enough pill to swallow. I still vividly remember what that classroom looked like that day. We still had an old overhead projector that revealed the shadows of our silhouettes. The lights were off, but the sunlight crept in from the window. A bob cut with

---

11   "Loving v. Virginia," Oyez, accessed April 25, 2020.

12   Ibid.

blond highlights framed my teacher's face. I remember turning around to my desk and feeling my heart race.

But everything was okay until I looked up and all of my classmates had so much to say.

"So... which race do you choose?" "What is your mom?" "What is your dad?" "Which race will you marry of the two?"

All I could think was my mom is a mom. My dad is a dad. Boys still have cooties. I am only in second grade. Everyone else knows just as much as I do. Who should I marry? Maybe you all should decide who.

I am not sure why the race of my future partner was one of the first things my fellow classmates wanted to know. I wish I had known that question would never go away though.

I didn't always know I would have to choose. Pick one. Identify with one more. I wanted to be both. I couldn't comprehend why it was so imperative for me to choose. Therefore, I would make it a point to always refuse. And when they asked, I would happily let them know I was both white and black. A perfect mix of the two.

# Token Black Friends

In the third grade, I had primarily white friends.

I would wear plaid shorts and New Balances. And no matter how I fixed it, my hair would always be considered nappy. I was just being me, which would often cause me to stick out like a sore thumb. Every time we went swimming, my hair would stretch out far and wide, reaching toward the sun.

My mom never wanted me to go swimming just after I got a relaxer. She wanted my hair to be pretty and manageable for at least a few days. And if you are unfamiliar, I would get chemicals put on my hair to straighten it out and make it more tamable. The number of times I had to explain this to my white friends is literally unfathomable.

They would say, "But please, just get in the pool with us. Your mom will never know," as if my afro wouldn't immediately snitch on me. But I'd still get in and wait until later to figure out how to explain. The pain I went through to get my hair done and my parents' money would go straight down the drain.

In the fourth grade, I got a new black best friend. And boy, let me tell you, this friendship would never end. I don't know if it was because we were both loud, outspoken, or couldn't get in the pool after relaxers. But I am sure it is because of a multitude of factors.

Our bodies were curvy, and our ambiance was felt in every room we entered. I guess this explains why our teacher made us sit out of recess so frequently. I had never gotten in any trouble before in my life. But it felt like my teacher was determined to make me think I was wrong, so sometimes I embraced my inner delinquency.

Maybe we did talk too much, think too much, had too much to say. Or maybe she liked us a little less because of our beautiful, brown skin. But either way, we'd make the best of our destiny on the sidewalk watching the other kids play. My teacher saved me from having to decide which kids it was okay to hang out with, and I liked it that way.

My teacher made us read the novel *Bud, Not Buddy* that year. She played the audiobook as our eyes traced the words on each page. Each chapter revealed a new message about race, poverty, and perseverance in the 1930s.[13] My eyes would race to the next section and then slow back down to the flow of the audio, allowing my ears to periodically catch up with my eyes but teaching my mind to wonder on its own, giving meaning to each message beyond what is shown.

---

13  Christopher Paul Curtis, *Bud, Not Buddy* (Delacorte Books for Adult Readers, 1999).

Can I make the accusation that my teacher treated the black girls differently since she assigned us such a book, a book full of black stories and black worries? I debate this with myself, but the answer is yes. I believe that oppressive biases and good intentions can exist at the same time. I don't think she intentionally looked at us black girls and immediately saw trouble. I think this world taught her to overanalyze our actions. This made us look less like little girls and more like distractions.

A Georgetown Law Center study states, "Black girls are viewed as less innocent and more adult-like than their white peers *at almost all stages of childhood* beginning most significantly at the age of five, peaking during the ages of ten to fourteen, and continuing during the ages fifteen to nineteen."[14]

We never had time to be girls when, at every age, the world saw grown women who were responsible for how everyone else perceived them. Our issues aren't self-inflicted; I can look back on my life and see exactly where they stem.

My best friend and I had hardworking parents and an uncharted amount of freedom. We were blessed with semi-safe neighborhoods and cell phones before we needed them. We spent summers together while our parents worked—blasting music from Paramore to Beyoncé, accepting every style, making videos, dance choreographies, and skits that let our imagination run wild.

---

14    Rebecca Epstein, Jamilia Blake, and Thalia González, "Girlhood Interrupted: The Erasure of Black Girls' Childhood," *SSRN Electronic Journal*, 2017.

We went to the mall alone at ten years old. It was a time just before the world got too dark for something like that. Our parents gave us each a crisp twenty-dollar bill, and we would be on our way—just enough money for a clearance outfit from Rue 21, a meal from American Deli, and maybe a matinee movie. Completely content with each other's company. Protecting each other as each grown man walked past us and gave us suggestive looks at such a young age. This was the birth of our uncontrollable, anti-misogynistic rage.

Together, we went through every traumatic event that took place, inherently feeling like grown women stuck in prepubescent bodies—not knowing that was actually our realities.

We allowed ourselves to be creative and expressive. We created a safe space where we didn't question our desire to listen to Carrie Underwood or Miranda Lambert. Our dialect didn't "fit" our identity. We had brown skin, but we knew that didn't have to limit our range. It would be the world that later taught us we were strange.

We saved our future selves by living our best life back then. We grew up, got lost, and found ourselves confused about who we were more times than we could count. But we can still dream of the little black girls we used to be—free of assumptions, standards, or stereotypes. We strive to be those girls again, the ones who drowned out the noise and stayed authentic to the souls within.

Before social media, our racial identity had yet to be turned into memes and funny things. My best friend and I would later become the token black friends. We had no idea that our actions, the way we dressed, and the way we spoke would soon become trends.

This shared experience may have saved my life. The world saw me as a little black girl, but I had no knowledge of the lens others saw me through. Raised by a white woman, I couldn't begin to understand my identity. But at least I wasn't alone in this experience.

I had a black best friend who was willing to be seen as disruptive and unruly with me until the end.

# PART THREE

# Middle School Drools

In the blink of an eye, I was in middle school attending honors and gifted classes. I don't think this was because I was smarter than anyone else, but I had the resources to do my homework in a quiet home and always had money in my lunch account. The stability at home made me successful in school, without a doubt.

I didn't work any harder to be put in these higher-level classes. I didn't work longer hours to be raised in a better neighborhood. I cannot claim my own attributes put me in these positions. I am merely a product of my conditions.

In sixth grade, my friend told me he often got beaten up at the bus stop in the mornings. I remember thinking this was weird. Or *funny*. I didn't know exactly how to feel, but I know I had no instinct that made me feel concerned. I didn't know what other neighborhoods were really like outside of mine. I'd say that's a privilege. Something purely out of my control; this was the life I was given.

As the rigor of my classes increased, I started to notice that my classrooms were really white, and I stuck out as the mixed kid even more. But that meant nothing to me at the time. Half of my family was white. My cousins wore camo and Confederate flag belts around their waists, which always secretly got under my skin, but I had yet to gain the skills to properly explain why. I know now that the Confederate flag still represents the oppression of black people—just another thing that screams white people are superior, another hate symbol that divides us by our exteriors.

My favorite classes that year were math and science. And little did I know, that was the year I would be taught compliance.

I was shy as a young child, but by the time I got into middle school, I was a social butterfly. For whatever reason, being a shy child in the world I lived in was simply never permitted. I had to greet everyone I encountered in black hair salons and was forced to mingle with old people in white churches. So over the years, all sorts of people picked and poked at me until I expressed myself—but definitely not in any ways that would be triggering. I had to simultaneously stay in a child's place, of course.

By the seventh grade, I thought I knew everything. I had so much to say about all the bad things, good things, and scary things—like feeling out of place as the only person of color in my granny's white circles, or the pressure to fit in with my white friends. I had so many thoughts about all the different things I saw and conversed about in these places—too many contradicting thoughts and too many paradoxical spaces.

During this time, everything began to feel unequal. So many things were always happening that I disagreed with or made me uncomfortable, but how would I utter the words that confirmed my disdain? How could I, just a little girl, dare to express the thoughts in my brain?

Instead, I made jokes with my friends, talked about boys, gossiped, made dance videos, recorded and posted fights on the bus. And when it came to my knowledge, only my teachers would know the depth of my mind. With every paper I turned in and each test I took, I always tried to do my very best. I could never play sports and didn't turn out to be a ballerina. In the classroom, I could learn and perform. My education was my art form.

My mother always reminded me to be thankful for my able mind and body. But in my pre-teenage mind, how I was doing in school was oh-so-unimportant. I was too busy spending time on Facebook chatting it up with my friends about who won *The Voice* or watching videos on YouTube about how to do my makeup because that dripped in importance.

My favorite science class that year was life science, and we were learning that organisms could reproduce, multiply. In special cases, they could even interbreed and create hybrid creatures. A lion and tiger could make a liger. A zebra and donkey could make a zonkey. And from the day the teacher introduced the topic, the white boys in my class would make sure everyone knew humans could interbreed too. A white woman and a black man could make an unnatural organism like me.

This kind of uncomfortable discourse became an everyday thing. Some of the white boys said they would never let their future white daughters be with a black man. They could be friends with "them," but nothing *too* extreme.

I always had a million thoughts and feelings rapidly shooting through my mind in these situations. Yet I never knew what to say, so I would get so upset or very hot and bothered while trying to find the right reaction. I hated they had the Power to make me feel less than, so I came up with whatever smart reply I could muster. We all know that teenage boys live to make girls mad, so I became the brunt of many of their jokes. Feeling like there was no other way out, I always had the exact reaction they wanted to provoke.

I think many people believed racism wouldn't be so blunt in the twenty-first century. But our divide was always presented to me so clearly. They didn't make these racist comments behind my back. They always made sure to say them to my face, and I will always be thankful for that.

Due to what felt like geographical imprisonment of living and growing up in South Georgia as a person of color, *hot and bothered* became my identity at this young, impressionable age. I was finally more than *just* the mixed girl or the face of what it means to be biracial. I was the Easily Offended, Often Times Bitter Mixed Girl. Quite the step up if you ask me.

By the eighth grade, I was filled with so many opinions, thoughts, passions, and rage that it did become who I was. I wanted nothing more than to capitalize on it. I fully committed to wearing my fury like a badge and using my brain as a weapon. This was the birth of what I like to call my Powerful expression.

I found my words that year—ones I could write down and even verbally express.

That year, only two teachers taught us all four subjects. One of my teachers taught both English and social studies, where she made us think, write, and argue until we all hated each other. She proved to me that writing could make me strong in any subject. She would sit at the front of the room and read our papers aloud. We cackled at each other's mistakes, got embarrassed, nearly humiliated, and never wanted to write anything ever again.

After that public humiliation, even without mentioning any names, my New Yorker teacher gave us a failing grade to make sure we knew for sure just how horrible we were at writing. And for a perfectionist who had to bring a report card home to certified hard workers, a failing grade wouldn't work for me. I felt called to rise to her standards, no matter what she demanded.

This is one of my very first teachers who wasn't born and bred in the state of Georgia. She recognized and unapologetically expressed that her so-called gifted and honors students struggled to write a good essay and couldn't even formulate a sufficient sentence. This kind of harsh criticism had enough Power to make you see yourself outside of your own "bubble" and grant yourself independence.

If I hadn't ended up in that class with that specific teacher, maybe I would still think it's okay to only use my brainpower to create strongly worded Facebook posts and never something as ambitious as a book. The combination of humility and perseverance is all it took.

I still feel pity sometimes when thinking about all the kids in other classes who got passing grades with misspelled words and plagiarized paragraphs. I feel bad that not one of their teachers took the time to correct them when they used the wrong your/you're or there/they're/their. Meanwhile, my teacher didn't just circle every mistake I made in red pen; she also came for me in class, and it *always* felt like an attack. She questioned me and filled me with doubt.

The best thing about it.... her skin was black.

In school, you learn about the same things over and over a thousand times. But learning about Georgia history and slavery from a Northern black woman revealed that there just may be more to uncover than my whitewashed, crumbling textbooks could tell me.

For the first time since kindergarten, I had a teacher who felt and looked like me. All the others were nice and sweet, but her stories were about black experiences and black sororities—black movies and black stories. She was an example of a strong, educated black woman I could feel, touch, and see. She was loud, and sometimes I wanted her to shut up. She was exactly who I wanted to be.

I still feel sorry for the black girls who never got to closely interact with a black woman in school—only ever getting teachers who would politely remind them that they should be quieter, follow the rules more closely, and definitely stop wearing the revealing clothes their parents worked so hard to buy them. I still feel sorry that they never witnessed a black woman who could be loud and bold but educated too. My insecurities whisper that maybe a full black girl instead of half black girl like me deserved it more too.

The principal of my middle school was also a black woman. She and my teacher were in rivaling black sororities, and the energy I felt when they were both in the room made me want to tell someone what to do. It made me feel like I could be a teacher, principal, CEO, and president too. I had already spent at least a decade on this Earth, and small things like these were just happening—making me feel like my dreams could come true.

One of my professors shared with me that "seeing someone who looks like some aspect of you as successful helps you believe you can do it too. If we are not accounting for everyone's experience through representation, we're leaving a lot of people out of that story."[15]

And Kenneth J. Meier said, "Recruiting black teachers can result in less second-generation discrimination against black students."[16] It's simple. If most of our teachers are

---

15    Dr. Joselyn K. Leimbach, interview with author, April 20, 2020.

16    Kenneth J. Meier, "Teachers, Students, And Discrimination: The Policy Impact of Black Representation," *The Journal of Politics* 46, no. 1 (1984): 261-262.

white women, teachers of other identities aren't being given a platform to be heard or give influence. We cannot learn or do things differently if we do not challenge these structures.

* * *

Finally, people who looked like me were thought leaders in my environment too. My teacher was black, and my principal was black, but still, none of us ever felt protected at school. Every single day that my female friends and I walked into our classroom, we waited quietly and patiently, as we were taught to do. And every single day, the males in our classrooms used their violent voices and manipulative tactics like they were taught to. Each of us girls waited our turn for the next comment about how our thighs were too large, our facial hair was revolting, and our girly feelings were annoying. You know, the perfect environment for adolescent thinking, learning, and growing.

We were surely not the first generation to experience bullying, but everyone tells us we are super-duper sensitive. I guess so. I mean, our bullying almost always followed us home—not in the car behind us or in the very back seat of the bus, but in our pockets and on our person. All it took was the unlocking of the cell phone or latest iPod Touch to learn about the next repulsive thing about you.

Or you might open an unwanted text and see your friend's nude photos that you never wanted to see because she sent it to a boy that she thought she trusted. It's easy to explore your body and sexuality with the internet at your fingertips— only to be labeled a slut when you walk by in the lunchroom, followed by being called a whore on an anonymous website when you get home from school, and confirmed with the word "thot" in your Instagram comments before you go to sleep. This happened so many times I don't have a specific friend in mind. It happened to them all. It never happened to me, but I was just bullied about being fat, overly emotional, and ridiculously tall.

Where were the adults when we needed them to guide and protect us? Probably online shopping or scrolling down Instagram too. Granted, things like iPhones and iPods were just then gaining traction. But how did the creators of the most innovative technology or the administrators of our schools not consider that the reality of the boys in our classrooms picking on us both in school and at home could be quite the distraction?

Low self-esteem and experiences with cyberbullying are directly correlated, making it imperative that educators intervene in these incidents because failure to do so can impact the ability of students to be successful at school.[17] We desperately needed the adults to help us feel validated, normal, and full.

But I guess that was the least of anyone's worries. So the world would go on, and one of my "thot" friends would be pregnant before we made it out of middle school. This time, I have a specific friend in mind. Everyone stared at her, judged her, and exclaimed how they would NEVER have sex until marriage—just doing what we were taught to do. Our teachers also passed

---

17    Justin W. Patchin and Sameer Hinduja, "Cyberbullying and Self-Esteem," *Journal of School Health* 80, no. 12 (2010): 614.

judgment instead of wondering why she didn't have access to a condom, birth control, or even the proper knowledge to avoid becoming an adult so early. Even our educators moved distastefully and showed us how to handle situations poorly.

Maybe protecting our mental or sexual health wasn't the job of the school. But in eighth grade, we learned that protecting us from being shot and killed at school was the least of anyone's worries too. We heard about Sandy Hook on the news where children as young as elementary schoolers failed to be protected while learning the alphabet and the different seasons. I knew I was just lucky because any day, I could hear a code red on the intercom and my brain could also turn bloody.

Therefore, in middle school, I started to take my education more seriously. I don't think I knew it would be the key to unlocking the door that could lead me out of all the madness, but I knew it could at least provide me with some answers. I knew I was lucky to be "gifted," to make it on the bus on time, and to end up with good teachers sometimes. I was even lucky to be taunted enough about my race to be filled with rage, and not given enough teachers who looked like me that when I did... *I would feel something*—enough of something to one day lead me to write things powered by the same kind of motivation that makes me want to fill each page.

Issues around race, sex, and safety will always fill my head with worries—breaking me down and covering me in hopelessness but sometimes building me up enough to allow me to share my stories.

# High School Fools

I wish I had more to say about high school but not much pops into my memory. I have to dig for things, which worries me that I blocked much of it out.

Going into high school, I was aware that the enrollment was split exactly in half between white and minority. I had yet to figure out if I was too white for the minority or too black for the majority. So I never actively tried to fit in with one or the other. In some ways, this made me Becky with the good hair—the annoying light-skinned girl who could actually ponder about who to hang out with without it being predetermined. My nice clothes, brand-new car, and what I would call "my-mother-is-white" privilege was enough for me to find my own place—although this does not mean I didn't subconsciously fight for this space.

My high school experience began in 2013 at Brunswick High School. I believe it carried the same charm it did on the day it was built in 1967. Constructed only a few years after desegregation, it still forced its students to coexist in the same ways. The aroma of many past lives and the growing mold brushed my face each time I entered the building. We could only fight over so many textbooks with missing pages, so we always had to sit and read closely with our neighbors. Then we proceeded to push classmates out of the way in the very tiny halls. But the outdated building always forced us back together again at lunch or made us sit nearly on top of each other at pep rallies.

Somehow, the ancientness of the building didn't bother us much. We didn't complain about the rotting walls or the peeling carpet. We could use glitter, paint freely, and ruin the building if we wanted—eat our snacks in class and attract more rats—the building was already haunted.

I only spent a few months in the deteriorated, historic building that both of my parents also attended. During my freshman year, a brand-new school was being built across the street. We were snatched from our first high school memories and placed in a building where we felt lost and confused all over again. But this time, there were stairs and large hallways—big windows and a courtyard the size of a football field. I remember thinking we were so lucky to be given new infrastructure to thrive in—lucky to get a building that would cost my community $57 million. I hoped a school set at that price would begin to produce a new, miracle community of scholars.

With about 60 percent of my school considered "economically disadvantaged," with heartbreakingly low rates of reading proficiency, that would simply be impossible.[18] Somehow,

18  "Brunswick High School Student Body," *U.S. News and World Report*, accessed May 8, 2020.

in our new school, the textbooks were the same old ones, and all of my teachers were still tired from their second jobs. But at least our building was state of the art.

There were over two hundred cameras, and no handles on the outside doors—to protect us from intruders, of course, or maybe to protect the world from us. I was never too sure. It felt like the added space created more room for fights to start, dreams to be crushed, and feelings to be hurt. No room was permitted for growth, learning, or changes of heart. A high school with a legacy of low graduation rates and all sorts of different hate would only carry its culture into a new space. And for those of us who wanted to get away, it was a race.

Each day I spent there, it began to feel more like a prison. For many of my classmates, it would be the building that gave them a head start.

Luckily, I had grown into who I was in this same sparsely populated Georgian town I had always been in. I went to high school with most of the same kids I went to elementary school with. People knew who I was, what I stood for, and the most important piece of information in a small rural place: *who my parents were.*

Believe me when I say I ran with this. I ran with the idea of people knowing me and semi-accepting me in my community until the day I left that town. I ran in student council elections. I ran toward internships. I ran so far that I ended up in fancy limos headed toward prom, after-parties that lasted all night, and situations that almost got me into a lot of trouble. I ran into the cops being called, unhealthy coping mechanisms, and drama-filled school days. I ran until I was granted the opportunity to actually run away—the ultimate escape, going off to college.

Among the people at the top of my class, this college thing became very competitive. We all yearned for new experiences, to do what everyone wants to do in a small, rural place—escape from the place that makes you feel boxed in and nearly cut off; hoping you might get the chance to leave this place, unlike your parents; dreaming of making a different life for yourself, your caretakers, and maybe even your grandparents.

I cried when I searched for the notable alumni of this high school because all I saw were athletes. While I am overjoyed for the alumni who made it to the NFL, I wondered why none of the alumni were CEOs, authors, directors, or congresspeople. Could it be because we weren't given the tools to pursue these kinds of opportunities? Is it outrageous to assume that each human is, in some way, bound to the success of their communities?

After I got over the sadness, I realized it did make sense. Often, only a talented few were nourished in class, and *that* was apparent. If you were good at a sport, your teacher often felt obligated to pass you, even if that meant you would never learn to read well or handle your money. Those things would be up to you to learn if you somehow ended up with millions of dollars and on an airplane in first class.

But how could I complain? Each NFL player conditioned at Brunswick High would give back to their community—provide a football training camp or maybe pay the school a visit—but never anything to help new minds grow.

The school parking lot was divided into different cliques. Many times, I heard people refer to one side as the "black side." I would roll my eyes, feeling aggravated after immediately realizing that I parked on the white side.

I am critical of the cliques now, but I wasn't then. I was one of the main perpetrators. I subscribed to the hierarchy without having any idea. The social norms were formed way before I came along. I was just a mindless teenager making others feel like they didn't belong. I knew the feeling so well, but I used it to test just how far I could be accepted.

I had friends I loved and who loved me like family. They accepted me into their white homes, and I went to their white Christmases. They felt so familiar to my white family, white mother, and white life. I started to forget I was any different than them.

The same black hairstylist did my hair since the fifth grade. I always got my hair done the same—relaxers then a flat iron to make sure my hair was bone straight. At some point, I stopped calling it a "flat iron" and referred to it as a "straightener" like my white friends—just little white lies and white adjustments to fit in, anything to diminish the discrepancies between us. Those adjustments never felt good or natural. They felt necessary or mandatory. My true self became collateral.

I showed my hairstylist pictures of the way I wanted my hair dyed—ombre, blond highlights. Each picture was of white women with hair completely different than mine. My hairstylist would say, "This won't look exactly the same because your hair is a different texture." This went in one ear and out the other, as I thought, *I don't need the lecture.*

I was completely lost, but I thought the exact opposite. I thought I had everything, or at least enough. I was in the popular crowd. I had friends and went to parties. But I always felt so empty, like no one could even hear me.

I was the crazy, loud, fun mixed girl of the group until I got tired. My best friend, the Token Black Friend, would pick up my slack sometimes and give me a break from being the entertainer—the outrageous one, the funny and creative one, the always-has-something-to-say-and-always-willing-to-share-their-hot-take one, feeling like puppets with our noses growing more and more every day.

In eleventh grade, we both started feeling the weight of our realities. Once we caught feelings for white boys, they shoved the truth in our faces. We were always the side chick, the late-night text, the cute face. Never the take-home, meet-your-parents kind of romance. Never the girlfriend or asked to the homecoming dance.

I guess plenty of girls don't have these experiences, but our situations drained us in unprecedented ways. We had boys gush over us in secret, refusing to let ourselves wonder if they didn't want to publicly show interest in a black girl, creating more self-esteem issues and self-hatred in our black world.

Of course, we could never be sure. The guys who liked us after hours and when no one else was around would go on to date white girls, while we wondered if our stomach size or loud laughs made them run away—trying our hardest to avoid the thought that maybe our brown skin or coarse hair kept them from wanting to stay.

Some boys would just say, "I don't like black girls," and we feared what they would say behind our backs if they would say that to our face. They claimed it was just a preference, but this preference assumes that all black girls are exactly the same. And out of all the millions of them, they could never be attracted to any of them.

We heard things like this every day, yet we still wonder why we feel insecure.

Most people loved and accepted us, but that didn't mean they weren't unknowingly doing things to oppress us. No one ever took up for us. They never spoke of police brutality or other issues that concerned the black community. They didn't even acknowledge that our struggles were different.

The saddest part? I allowed it. If I pushed it on them, would they have cared? I doubt it.

The girls and gays recognized a small inkling of this kind of pain. My white girlfriends never went out of their way to stand up to their blatantly racist families or defend us in class, but they loved me for who I was without hesitation. The thing is, all girls know in their core what it's like to be judged, stereotyped, and ridiculed.

The same was true for my gay friends, both in the closet and out. While people who looked like me were being called "niggers," people called them "faggots" to their faces. They could always connect with me in ways we didn't even have to speak on. We had an underlying understanding. We clung to each other as we blasted our eclectic music, shared our depths of hearts, and started drama with anyone who dared to cross us.

Over time, it became the girls and gays against the boys. We tried our best to uplift each other and drown out the negative straight male noise.

I started to resent anyone who I viewed as being "in opposition" to me or my identity. My friends and I used the word "opps." For me, most boys were the opps. My teachers were the opps. The police were the opps. My parents were the opps. Self-proclaimed "republicans" in my classes were the opps. And anyone who went to the only other high school in our town, Glynn Academy, were the opps of ALL opps. So every time we had a sporting event against them, I pulled out all of my tricks, while the entire town would get ready for the show and grab their chips.

I did anything to get this anger out of me and onto someone else. So if it was time for a Brunswick High vs. Glynn Academy football game, I was the first to spark up some overdramatized rivalry that started way before my time.

Since my generation was gifted with powerful tools like Twitter, this was extremely easy for me. Our football team sucked most years, but that never stopped me from tweeting something like, *Can't wait to show Glynn Academy what we are about on Friday.* I chose something that lacked aggression but was just enough to poke at someone's pride. Of course, the Glynn Academy kids took this as an attack, and from there, I just hung on for the ride.

While we argued with each other on Twitter, it became less about football and more about identity. It's sad for me to even think about because now I know we must have been so full of hurt and hatred. I was never the type to make fun of someone for their appearance, but I always had a rebuttal for whoever came for me or my high school. I loved to pour gasoline on the fire, but the fire always grew way bigger than I desired.

They called us Brunswick High kids trashy, poor, illiterate, dirty—anything they could think of to berate a school with lots of black kids and low funding. We called them rich, spoiled, cocaine-addicted nuisances. Our comments never really hit the same. The reality of our words didn't even register to any of us. Our insensitive remarks revealed that we were completely aware of the inequality around us and ignorant of it at the same time—pointing fingers that pointed back at us, pushing along the agenda and enabling the system formed against us.

This happened every year of high school, but my junior year was worse than all the others. I was such a dramatic person by this point, mostly because everyone else taught me this was who I should be. I quickly found myself as the face of my high school's drama, and it began to surround me. Some of the jokes were innocent, like when kids photoshopped my face on corn to make fun of my last name. But then they took pictures of my license plate that read "CAMCOBB" and send it in their group chats, calling me a "bitch" or "fat" or whatever else they could come up with. The screenshots got right back to me, but I was so numb to these kinds of comments that I really didn't even care. I couldn't feel anything anymore. In my inflated teenage brain, their comments were totally a bore.

But one picture took things too far. My face was photoshopped on a woman who was picking corn and cotton, reminding me of the black girl I was to them—not half-white, mixed, or biracial.

These people didn't know me personally, so my "mother-is-white" privilege couldn't save me. I knew my experiences were clearly different from white people, but I thought in some ways I was accepted enough—in ways that would save me from being seen as a slave. But I was reminded I was black in America. I guess I should've just shut my mouth and behaved.

Some people saw how messed up that image was, but many said nothing—didn't take up for me, didn't express any kind of outrage. I posted it on Facebook to get the parents involved and exploit the racism that still existed in our town. Enough people from the other school reported my post, where I begged for justice or an acknowledgment, that it was eventually taken down. I don't know why I thought I had any chance of bringing light to such a subject in my unchanging town.

I would never forget days like that. This is why I woke up every day feeling defeated, disrespected, and unwanted. I wanted nothing more than to get out of that town full of racist white people—people who woke up every day to judge and scrutinize others all while going on about how they "don't see color."

My annoyance turned into the highest level of resentment. I finally learned that in no reality could the place that built me also support me. Somehow, I was born in a town and a state where black slaves came after being yanked from another continent and were forced to build the foundations of our ecosystem. I finally accepted that those same sick mentalities would outlive the desegregation, the building of new schools, and the cultivation of new foundations.

Behind each door of the homes of my town, outdated ideologies would still be blooming.

# Senioritis

I was diagnosed with senioritis the moment my junior year ended. My motivation for school went straight out the window. I say this while I had a 4.0 GPA, but that made me feel even more entitled to a break.

My grand escape from my hometown was so close that I could taste it. I applied to as many colleges in my state as possible because my scholarship only covered in-state tuition. I tried to keep my mind away from what other people were doing and stay away from the idea of it being a competition.

The moment I got into the "college of my dreams," the University of Georgia, my thoughts and dreams expanded so far outside of what that tiny town had been selling me.

But I am not sure that was ever my dream college. It was just that the red Georgia "G" popped up all over my home. Georgia games were played in every restaurant in my town, and everyone I knew considered themselves a Dawg fan. Dreaming of ivy leagues or schools in big diverse cities never even crossed my mind. Somehow, I still thought I was exiting the echo chamber, but boy, I was blind.

All my classmates also yearned for new experiences, and my dream wasn't so different from everyone else's. So among our small cohort of gifted and honors kids, it was an undercover competition. Each of us was more than ready to fight for our right to pay for overpriced tuition.

The chatter of who was accepted to different colleges and universities quickly filtered into all of our pretentious AP class conversations, yet it was rarely followed by admiration or congratulations. It was soaked in jealousy and comparison of applications. We all passed judgment, forgetting that we were making moves that could change our families for generations.

I was lucky to be accepted into a school that many of my classmates and I longed to go to. My decent test scores and a high GPA carried me along the way. But the moment people found out about my acceptance, it was no longer about the rigor of my classes but all about race.

I wish I could say my integrated high school provided me with different reactions from my classmates. In retrospect, my opportunities were better than my grandma's, who had to attend the first and only all-black high school in my town. I wish I could say that, decades later, the culture wouldn't be the same exact way. But things remained the same from my elementary school memories to my high school days.

Once I got into UGA, I was reminded of how my peers saw me. Some said I was smart and had something special. Some teachers said they didn't know I had it in me. But of course, I was reminded that the Easily Offended, Often Times Bitter Mixed Girl is who I would always be.

People I considered my closest friends looked me in my face and said my mind hadn't gotten me into my dream university. Because their white minds weren't accepted and my biracial brain was, it was obviously affirmative action, and colleges only wanted me to improve their diversity.

This same sweet reminder taunted me during all of my years of schooling—the hidden message that I wasn't allowed to be educated and black. It had to be one or the other. Even if I spent nights at their white homes and their parents hugged me, I would always be too mixed for our minds to be equal.

* * *

This was my senior year—the year 2016, to be exact. That year would be full of surprises. I was preparing to become an adult. That year, I was accepted into college, I made my last memories with my life-long friends, and my "mother-is-white-privilege" allowed me to sometimes capitalize on my complexion. But most importantly, it was the year of the 2016 election.

By that point, I was completely infatuated with politics. *Scandal* was my favorite show, and I had a crush on a boy who wanted to be a lawyer. I dreamed about being a politician one day, so everything began to be about politics for me. In fact, I don't remember anything else from the year 2016. All I remember is refreshing the screen, staring at the television, shifting my eyes back and forth from my phone to the TV, pinching myself, wondering if my reality was as bad as it seemed.

Donald Trump became the President of the United States.

Now, I should make it perfectly clear that this had nothing to do with my political affiliations. Parties do not matter to me, and frankly, I see the government for what it is—the government. George Washington was definitely on to something when he said, "A division of the republic into two great parties… is to be dreaded as the great political evil."[19] Therefore, let's talk as if parties didn't exist in this world—in the sense that all of my opinions and observations are the result of my experiences, never to mirror the political party I tend to identify with when I share things on Facebook. In my world of politics, I play by my own playbook.

Donald Trump was the last person I ever thought would *actually* become the president. He is the last person anyone thought would even run for president.

I remember scrolling through Twitter, where so many people thought it was a freaking joke. TV reality star from *The Apprentice*, businessman, and trust-fund receiver, Donald Trump, was running for president of the United States of America. What a funny joke. It was truly meme-worthy. We'd never elect someone who radiated such hostility. It was hard to imagine with the Obama-era comfortability.

---

19   Lee Drutman, "America Is Now the Divided Republic the Framers Feared," *The Atlantic*, 2020, Accessed May 8, 2020.

It was funny until it was real. And it became more real with every rally that popped up in each new swing state. It became more real the more I saw him on TV and on my smartphone. It became more real every time I heard my classmates chat about him in class or coworkers rant about the election. And as you can imagine, in a small semi-rural town in South Georgia, the reviews were outstanding. In my little mixed and confused mind, I couldn't figure out what I was misunderstanding.

I watched almost every single person in my small town become Donald Trump's biggest fan. And let me tell you, this is a young colored girl's biggest nightmare. It was more than constantly seeing the red Make America Great Again hats. More than the rednecks at my high school feeling more comfortable than ever to run their Confederate flags up and down the school parking lot. And it was a hell of a lot more than yet another privileged white man coming just that close to becoming the new leader of the free world.

It was more about the fact that he didn't even have the right qualifications. He was not qualified enough to be in the position to run for such a role in our government. In terms of education and experience, he surely didn't match up to his competitors. This was proof to me that it didn't matter how educated I became. The white man would always have easier access to the world. I doubted I could have a future in politics. Maybe black girls have a better chance of becoming cashiers, janitors, or cosmetologists.

It was more about the fact that he would go on national television and call Mexicans drug dealers, criminals, and rapists. All this time, I believed that Mexicans could also be doctors, lawyers, and U.S. representatives. The narrative was changing. This proved to me that no matter what complexion of non-white you were—Chinese, Vietnamese, Native American, Indian, African, Black—you were susceptible to becoming the white man's target. Anyone could be picked to be the brunt of their white anger. It was a lot worse than I thought, and I was in even more danger.

It was more about the video evidence of the man running for president saying the words, "Grab 'em by the pussy. You can do anything." I thought there was no way anyone would want someone with this kind of moral compass to be the next president of the United States. This was proof to me that men could act however they please. They could be misogynistic, perverted, and disrespectful but still have the same opportunities as anyone else—making my colorful seventeen-year-old-girl dreams melt.

Donald Trump did and said some of the most horrific and degrading things while persuading people to be in favor of him. And it worked. He acted like your typical white privileged racist man and still had supporters. I watched him go up in ratings every day as he attacked certain groups of people. Often saying things that didn't even make sense or getting flustered like an immature child who didn't get his way. In my teenage brain, it just didn't make sense. But I couldn't vote, and everyone constantly reminded me of this when I tried to form an opinion. I felt like I was quickly surrounded by a bunch of Trump's little minions.

So there I was, feeling helpless. I couldn't even vote for the first female Democratic party nominee. I couldn't even vote for the other candidate, who probably wouldn't do anything for me or my community. But at least Hillary Clinton wasn't a complete threat to my entire identity.

There I was, feeling helpless, rambling about what would happen when Hillary Clinton and Donald Trump went face to face, making assumptions about who would win the presidency and what they would do with all that Power. I had no idea what the future had in store.

You know what happened next. He won. The white boys taunted me in class every day and said I was nothing but a stupid libtard. It was all in good loving fun though, right? They could never understand how devastating that election was to me. They didn't have to consider what it meant for undocumented people, people of color, women, or the LGBTQ+ community. Why would they care when they lived in a world that granted them full immunity?

My high school English teacher described the day after the election as the hardest day she ever had to teach. She said it was hard to walk into school when the country had let down so many of her black and brown students, while the rest of our town basked in their imprudence.

This is when I knew I'd be fighting for my rights for the rest of my life, begging my peers to join me. We are the only ones who can change these things for new generations to come. Once again, by we, I mean Generation Z or whoever we claim to be—the young people, the college students, the Instagram influencers, and everyone in between.

# PART FOUR

# First-Year Tears

This is the one where I finally went to college. I finally moved five hours away from the stinky, sometimes charming, little town I was born in. I gotta say… I absolutely, positively thought that was the moment my life would change forever. Spoiler alert: it was not. All those dreamy ideas about college would come to rot.

I packed up all my stuff in just a few days before heading off on my big new journey, eager to move out of the tiny house I'd lived in my entire life—the same house I crawled in, walked in, talked in, and cried in. But none of this came to mind when it was time to leave. I was so eager to see the new places I could make my home. I couldn't wait to find new, safer places for my mind to roam.

So I left South Georgia where the towns were small and the community was questionably tight-knit and entered what felt like an *entirely new world*… North Georgia. Yes, this is exactly where I played myself. I have no idea why I thought moving across the state would change the dynamics of my entire life and provide me with completely different results than the past eighteen years. I was young with the highest hopes of all hopes and committed to the idea of the life-changing college experience that was sold to me.

I always envisioned the moment that I hopped out of the "yeehaw" land and off to college as the moment I would also jump into a land where everyone supported not only my identity but everyone's existence. Considering I imagine everything in life like some kind of weird chick flick or scripted reality TV show, I was overwhelmingly disappointed from the rip. North Georgia was just like South Georgia, just in its own country ways. I walked out of a bubble and popped into another one, but this one was the home of the University of Georgia.

The University of Georgia is located in Athens, Georgia, and is the home of one of the best SEC college football teams. In so many ways, this place was strategically built and planned to provide the proper college experience. But no one told me that my dream college would be more like the setting and plot of the movie *Neighbors* with Zac Efron. Athens is basically one big tailgate party. For young adults looking to party, this place is a magnet. For business owners, realtors, and even Uber drivers—it is the place to be, because in the South, everybody, and I mean errrrbody, knows about the Georgia Bulldogs.

I naively leaped into this new environment feeling like I was rid of all the things I carried around with me at home... but I set myself up for failure with these unrealistic expectations, hoping to be free of the pressure to fit in while also standing out. Somehow, I genuinely thought things would be mostly sunshine and rainbows, but the little things started to rain on my parade from the get-go.

Before I even attended my first class, I had joined so many UGA group chats and Facebook groups over the summer that I got my feelings hurt really early. These groups consisted of young college students, primarily incoming freshmen, who were just as excited as I was about attending our new university. We all talked about what our majors would be, and we even found our roommates through these devices. And since we were in Georgia, you best believe all the girls were talking about what they would wear to sorority rush.

I mean, how else would you make friends? Greek life at UGA makes up about one-quarter of the student population.[20] Here's the breakdown: Greek life, athletes and sport enthusiasts, nerds, hippies, and black people. Obviously, there are many kinds of people on campus, and they all make up their own heterogeneous subsets. But there was a very clear black people sector. There was no question about that.

In fact, the black community on campus referred to themselves as "BUGA" to represent Black UGA. Cute, right? I thought so too, and naturally, I really wanted to be a part of it. I thought, FINALLY! I could join people whose world looks a little bit more like mine. It was finally my time to shine.

And of course, the BUGA class of 2021 group chat was popping. I remember when I found out that group chat existed, and I was yet to be added. I thought they just forgot about me,

---

20  Mary T. Moore, "UGA Fact Book 2018, 50th Edition," Oir.Uga.Edu, 2018.

or maybe they didn't realize I was black. But that was okay, I am used to that. So I didn't mind asking to be included. I was so used to being the Easily Offended, Mixed Girl brat.

Unfortunately, this would be the very first time the black community shut me down. To be fair, I didn't try many times to shoot my shot with black people prior to this, because I lived in my little ole South Georgian distorted world where I created my own biracially problematic space. But this time, the psychographics were different. I asked them to add me to the BUGA group chat, and they told me, "Nah, we're good," in more forms than I have ever heard it presented. In more unique and hilarious ways than I have ever been tormented.

It was, and I quote, "No, make your own MUGA." Mixed UGA. Clever. It was, "Nope, you are more white. We already figured that out," to "Girl, we don't want you," and even things like, "Nah, Oreo." I can laugh about this now, but at the time, I was so damn frustrated that people were attempting to deny me of my identity yet again that I felt like I would lose my mind.

Because my small rural town had ignited so much fire within me when it came to who I was, I individually messaged every single one of them about how they could never tell me anything about who or what I am. If this was a messed-up experiment to test just how black I was, I probably gave them way more than they actually wanted. And of course, once again, I began to think my world would always be haunted.

My new college community was supposed to be different. But this was the first sneak peek that everything would be the same. Therefore, I did what I'd always done—tried to fight to create my own space. I made a swift switch from Team Black People, who absolutely did not want me, to Team Greek Life, who would ultimately not want me.

Sorority rush was the week before classes started. I moved into my dorm early and woke up at the crack of dawn to get ready for the first day. I knew this would be like a weird *Mean Girls* dystopia, but I genuinely thought I understood the science of the white girl by this point. For some reason, I thought being raised by a white woman and surrounded by them my entire life would allow me to connect with them on at least a surface level. I mean, how else would I make friends? I thought I could endure four more years of ignoring their insensitive jokes and keeping up with their ever-changing trends.

That kind of outlook landed me in old mansions previously owned by white supremacists that had been flipped into sorority houses. I made my way around, talking to girl after girl I felt absolutely no connection to. I looked around and saw no one like me. After so many conversations about where I have vacationed or where my earrings were from, it wasn't hard to figure out that they weren't looking for girls like me. It actually didn't take any conversation for me to figure that out, I could simply tell by representation. I frantically looked around each house I entered to see if the sorority had any women of color. As I went from house to house, I was further disappointed; the number of brown girls would dwindle more and more.

I saw a few of my Token Black Girls and Bitter Mulatto Sisters strung throughout the houses like accessories, but there was never enough color to actually shatter the white supremacy that built up each of these sororities' histories.

I am not very good at the whole "fake it till you make it" thing, so I was already done with sorority rush by lunchtime on the first day. While the other girls gossiped about their top sorority choices, I was already in my car driving off. How would I make friends now? That was no longer any of my business. "You don't need friends to do well in college," my consciousness screamed. It is one of the times I actually appreciated my impulsiveness.

The more I tried to find a niche, clique, or cult at my new school, the more I realized that was actually the problem. I didn't have to fight for my place in a group, which was never what I wanted. I did not have to subscribe to this world that was only black, white, or haunted.

* * *

I finally began classes at the nation's first state-chartered university. The buildings were built by slaves while the brochures screamed diversity. The place where I was expected to learn and grow radiated the same kind of dissonance I had been so familiar with before. It began to feel like it would never go away; wherever I went, there would always be more.

In the first year, I made a few friends but not many. One friend was from my hometown. She ended up in my college town for a little while due to one of the annual tornadoes carried by climate change into the coast of Georgia.

I had always known who she was, and we frequently saw each other around over the years. I always wondered why she and her white brother looked so different, but all I knew was that she had dark hair and beautiful caramel skin that kind of looked like mine. She exerted the same kind of racially confused energy I had, one that you could not define.

I later learned she was Mexican and adopted into a white family. Being brown girls raised by white moms was a connection that quickly made us like family. We were lost and confused, yet so bold and sure of ourselves at the same time. Neither of us had found our place yet, so we were just enjoying the world in the meantime.

The closer we got, the more her story continued to unfold. She was born in a jail in El Paso, Texas after her mother was detained while trying to cross the border into the big, great United States of America. She became an orphan of the state of Texas and was adopted at just two years old. In many ways, this was the perfect age to be assimilated. Many people would probably say she is lucky to be adopted, and that cannot be debated.

She has always radiated an incredible joy for life. Anyone who has ever met her can sense that she is thankful for everything that landed her the life that she has. But the more I got to know her, the more I noticed the sadness behind her eyes and the wariness she felt about her past. There was no question that she was blessed, but she had never met a single member of her biological family and wasn't sure who she actually was. I had to dig for this because it was never part of her own expression. Because I related to that in so many ways, I was constantly asking questions.

She was an anomaly. Her views confused me, and her story intrigued me. I was learning so much from her; it didn't matter that we didn't always agree.

Just the year before, she voted for Donald Trump. I was flabbergasted to hear this. How could a Mexican person be a Trump supporter? Left-leaning, often hypocritical people who I closely identified with always tried to crucify her the moment they found out. But somehow, I found it in me to never judge her. It didn't make any sense, so I just tried to understand her.

I didn't get how she could vote for someone committed to deporting people from our country—people just like her. It was hard for me to know she contributed to young children being separated from their families who they would likely never see again. I wondered how she could side with the people who would ultimately create the same kind of distance she felt from her biological family. But I knew I could not judge her; I could only try to understand her story.

I learned that she didn't vote for Trump because she wanted to hurt people like her. She simply was not aware of the implications of her tiny act of democracy. It was more about making her adopted family proud—the one that raised her and put a roof over her head all these years. It was never about the biological family she did not know but about those who loved her, disciplined her, grew with her, and ordered her. She never had much of a choice. It was what she was supposed to do. It was only right. It didn't matter that she was brown and they were white.

And that is how I finally understood. I never wanted to be the black liberal sheep at my white Christmases either. I chose to be, but that was my own personal choice. Sometimes it felt like it would be much easier to just say and think nothing at all and go with their flow. It is so much harder to continuously swim against it. But I am privileged enough to know my family is blood, and they couldn't get rid of me if they wanted to. I could never blame her for simply supporting and aligning with the family she was adopted into.

She taught me everything I needed to know about the importance of understanding. Other people's reasoning didn't have to make sense to me, and they were entitled to do what they pleased. Over time, we would grow and learn so much from each other just by listening, laughing, crying, dancing, and never attacking. It could have been a scenario where I acted as I did in the past—unavailable, unwilling to listen, refusing to empathize—doing the same things as the people I bash.

None of us are forced to fit into any red or blue box. We make that choice for ourselves. No black or white group chat will make us feel like we are a part of something. And surely no sorority house or college campus can save us from our own harmful stereotypes and judgments.

But there are millions of people around us we don't understand, waiting for us to look them in the face. Then they will begin to act as a mirror, surprising you with each image and reflecting the same biases you have... making things so much clearer.

# Second-Year Fears

I slid out of my first-year jitters, confusion, and fun quite gracefully. I packed up my stuff yet again, moved out of my shoebox dorm room, and entered an unwanted but much-needed summer at home. While everyone else was eager to travel and finally catch some sunlight, I knew I would feel like a failure if I didn't go home and continue to work every fiber in my body. My mind was exhausted, so it was time for a break—a questionable switch to manual labor, just those unrealistic, first-generation expectations coming to play.

I became a server for this short period as I anxiously awaited my next semester. This experience provided me with the most humbling lesson about what it means to really *serve* others. I went into it thinking, *How hard could it really be?* And I left that summer thinking Waiting Tables 101 should be a course in college. Maybe it shouldn't be mandatory to feel dehumanized, overworked, and blamed for anything from a long wait time to an accidental piece of lettuce. But there was something beautiful about being forced to work as a team under such conditions—a team of single mothers, chain-smoking old ladies, hopeful immigrants, angsty teenagers, and other very annoyed college students. While we seemed to be at constant war in some ways, it was, undoubtedly, an array of hardworking humans.

I made so much money that summer but hardly saw a dollar of it. When my second year of college started, all the money I managed to save went directly to my first month of rent. Affordable housing in a gentrified college town is nearly non-existent, but it was important that I learned what it is like to work to survive, especially when well over half of my country is living paycheck to paycheck.[21] One of the few things in life that is all-inclusive—a sick destiny for the college grads, blue-collar workers, hood rats, and even rednecks.

I believe that summer job forced me to return to college with a new outlook. Because of that specific job in combination with the fact that every year as I get older, it feels like ten years of new lessons and epiphanies. My future and the way I fit in the world became a prominent thought in my mind. Thinking about how fast that first year went by, I knew it wouldn't be long before I would have a degree and enter the workforce. The reality of college started to set in.

In the first semester of my second year, my classes aligned in the most impactful way. I had Spanish, American history, macroeconomics, and women's studies. Unfortunately, the only thing that I learned from Spanish was that I was incredibly dyslexic, and it was a miracle I even made it this far in academia.

---

21   Zack Friedman, "78% of Workers Live Paycheck to Paycheck," *Forbes*, 2019, accessed May 9, 2020.

In American history, I learned the same facts I had learned at least five times prior in my life. But somehow, the truth of things like the Vietnam War and the Civil Rights movement made waves in my brain in ways they never did in my public school. I started to feel even more betrayed by the Georgia Department of Education because all these years, they withheld the juiciest information. Their curriculum never properly exposed me to the art of social movements, the way they brought all kinds of passionate people together from white hippies to black students. I could see myself in those people. It may have been the first time I ever saw parts of myself in history.

In macroeconomics, I learned that college would continue to be hard and I should probably learn how to study. I pushed out the most hard-won B I have ever earned, and I learned what was happening every time my classmates and I bought things on Amazon. Supply and demand are exactly why they don't allow their employees bathroom breaks. It finally made sense why Jeff Bezos holds such a large portion of the world's wealth. He has a flawless business model that focuses specifically on profit and ignores all else, like his employees' health.

And last but surely not least, women's studies taught me that I was black.

Now, you would think that nineteen years of living in a nonwhite body would have taught me this, but I know now that I had no idea what it meant to be black before taking this class. Obviously, I knew I wasn't white all this time, and I was aware of some ways the color of my skin made my life feel and look different than my white counterparts. But I had let the reoccurring notion that mixed-race people would always be "too black for the white people and too white for the black people" define my reality. I am not sure exactly when, but at some point, I simply accepted that. It was overdue that I reject it. I could be half-white without it taking away from my blackness. I think I convinced myself they canceled each other out like a math equation. Or the influx of the white creamer in my black coffee took me from a sophisticated, energizing morning drink to a childish, over-sweetened treat. No matter which underlying metaphor I actually felt about my race, it was toxic. It took my white, queer female women's studies teacher to show me that I was black. And we all know that once you go black, you never go back.

I had no idea that I was black because I had been the Easily Offended, Often Times Bitter Mixed Girl for so long, which was constantly reinforced throughout my life with the "half-white, half-black" agenda. I wasn't "full" of anything, didn't belong anywhere, and didn't relate to anyone. I had always known this wasn't true, but my idea of racial identity was so far from what it needed it to be.

I had learned how to look at myself and my race in the American South, where the history of the most brutal treatment of African Americans was cultivated, maintained, and preserved; where the oldest folk could still vividly remember segregated schools and colored water fountains; where the number of sick ideologies and racist ways of thinking they taught their children were countless.

I have never existed in a world where I could have a black thought without vicious white interruption, whether from a teacher, a friend, or the woman who raised me. This women's studies professor connected me with literature and stories from women with all sorts of different cultural backgrounds, generational differences, and geographical barriers—each of them sharing with me another tool to start figuring out my racial identity. I had been so confused about it my entire life, but this didn't stop me from coming to different conclusions about who I was over the years. Each conclusion lacked the proper analysis of my black fears, my black tears.

I knew what racism, colorism, and inequality meant to me, but I lacked the knowledge of what it meant to my entire black community.

Books like *This Bridge Called My Back* and *Women, Race, and Class* blew my mind. I learned of the deeply and strategically ingrained oppression of women of color. I learned of the undercover superpower of being both black and a woman. I learned that the people who were historically brought down only rose high above the shitty outcomes expected of them. These stories from women of color obliterated all the knowledge I thought I had into tiny little pieces. This knowledge was the soil that gave the seeds of my experiences room to sprout. It truly allowed each thought and opinion in my black female mind to grow with everlasting potential; in ways that would be endlessly influential.

* * *

I was soon sucked back into the world of politics with the upcoming gubernatorial Georgia election, but this time, I had an entirely new sense of who I was and what I stood for.

It filled me with so much joy and excitement that one of the candidates was a black woman—a black woman willing to prove that if she could become the first black female governor in the United States, I could too. Her name was Stacey Abrams. She wasn't skinny. She wasn't quiet. She wasn't doing the things expected of a woman, thus fueling my dream of being a congresswoman.

Once again, I became so obsessed and emotionally invested in this election that I could not think straight. It was gaining national attention because the fight between red and blue in America had turned into a series of battles. I mean, this was now the Trump era. For this to all be popping off in my home state of Georgia, I didn't even know what to think.

I saw Stacey speak at a coffee shop in my college town. I remember reflecting on the turnout after leaving that day, feeling like she could actually freaking win. I had longed for this kind of attention and much-needed progressive change in my state for so long. But as the people in my state always seemed to do, they would prove me wrong.

Wrong. Liar. Stupid. Delusional. Naïve. I was all those things as soon as I began to express my support for Abrams. Many people from my hometown called me insane for wanting to vote for someone so "crooked." Wasn't that the same thing they called Hillary? The way politics worked in the South was so beyond me.

Stacey Abrams was unarguably more qualified than her opponent. She had studied public policy at both an undergraduate and graduate level, then earned her Juris doctorate.

She served in the Georgia House of Representatives and later became the minority leader.[22] And her opponent? I'll put it simply—he was a cheater.

Brian Kemp received his bachelor's—his only degree—in Agriculture from none other than the University of Georgia. I am sure Mr. Kemp is an expert in crops and tractors, but that didn't prove to me he was qualified to be head of our state. Public schools, city funding, traffic laws, and any other state regulation completely relies on the decisions made in the State Capitol. Georgia may have a lot of farms, but that is just one sector affected by our state legislation. He did not even come close to Abrams when it came to proper education.

Race is beside the point in this specific gubernatorial race if you can look over the fact that a black woman attorney was constantly being dragged down and completely shat on in comparison to her white farmer opponent. Georgians made it clear to me that farming was so important that it completely qualifies you to run the internal functions of the entire state. But to me, that was certainly a debate.

Now, Mr. Kemp was also the secretary of state in Georgia at the time, which could possibly give him some brownie points if you disregard the fact that he was the man in charge of elections.

He started by purging 107,000 inactive voters from registration in one historic day, just a start to the game to guarantee

---

22   "Meet Stacey | Stacey Abrams For Governor," Join Stacey Abrams, 2018, accessed May 9, 2020.

previously inactive (mostly minority) voters couldn't have a say in this race. [23] In 2017 alone, 600,000 Georgia voters were purged under Kemp.[24] How could that make sense? Being in charge of elections while running in one? I have no idea, but it seems to me that making logical sense in this kind of state is nearly an arrestable offense.

Brian Kemp had commercials and ads all over the place with him driving a truck and holding a gun, saying he would "round up criminal illegals." I wish I was kidding. He said, "If you want a politically incorrect conservative, that's me."[25] So he warned us he didn't care much for good politics or the lives of the immigrants who work on our very farms and rural land. But gaining support from other fascists, who refuse to accept the fact this entire country is stolen land in the first place, is not actually how he won. On election day, Kemp had the most fun.

Abrams had already expected her opponent's campaign to function unfairly, so her campaign organized voters in ways my state had never seen. People who had refrained from being politically involved were registering to vote, feeling more inspired than ever.

But on election day, our secretary of state made sure necessary cords and voting machines never showed up—creating

---

23  Hannah Knowles and Reis Thebault, "Georgia Purged 309,000 Voters from Its Rolls. It's the Second State to Make Cuts in Less Than a Week," *The Washington Post*, 2019, accessed May 9, 2020.

24  Khushbu Shah, "Textbook Voter Suppression: Georgia's Bitter Election a Battle Years in the Making," *The Guardian*, 2018, accessed May 9, 2020.

25  "Brain Kemp: 'So Conservative'—Campaign 2018," Video, *The Washington Post*, 2018, accessed May 9, 2020.

lines to vote that took hours that working people could not afford to lose, not counting absentee ballots that ensured college students and world travelers' votes would not be counted.[26] In all, 53,000 votes would not be counted due to Kemp's "exact-match" policy, and of course, 70 percent of these voters were black.[27] The right to vote that our ancestors fought so hard for could be stripped away easier than I thought. Tweets and articles filled my timeline about the Georgia governorship and voter suppression. I was filled with rage but too entirely familiar with my state's unfortunate trend of oppression.

I got my hopes up thinking the United States could have its first black female governor—one who experienced poverty and was the valedictorian of her public school. I should've known from all my past experiences that girls like me never win—not when we are fighting against private school-bred, suburb-raised white men. Georgia wasn't the place for this kind of change—not during the Trump era, not during a time when the only familiar emotions are fear, hatred, and terror.

I carried this disappointment around with me for the next few months. I started to feel trapped in one place—weighed down by the lack of progress in my country, my state, and my communities. So I used this feeling of hopelessness to help me run away for just a little while. I applied to study abroad, which a first-generation student would never dare to do. I was really pushing it by making this leap, and I had never even

---

26   John Haltiwanger, "Georgia Voters Face Long Lines, Malfunctioning Voter Machines Amid Hotly Contested Governor's Race," *Business Insider*, 2018, accessed May 9, 2020.

27   Ibid.

been on an airplane before in my life. But an escape from my American reality sounded nice.

On a Social Work and Women's Health directed study, I explored the land of Grenada—a tiny country most people never hear of. Even though the United States had invaded the little defenseless country under Reagan, Grenadians probably know more about American politics than Americans do. Over the course of a week, this country and its culture impacted me in ways I'll never forget.

Grenada met me exactly where I was. Its beaches and palm trees reminded me of my beach bum town in Georgia. But its welcoming spirit taught me something new. Not only was it the most beautiful place I had ever seen, but it was also filled with the kind of community and pride I had never experienced—a country where most of the population are descendants of African slaves. Somehow, after being colonized by nearly every major force in the world, it kept its rich black culture intact. The colorful houses, braided hair, flavorful food, energetic music, and kind souls felt like home to me. Somewhere I had never been before and thousands of miles away from where I grew up felt more like home than I had ever experienced. It taught me that the meaning of home changes with each ounce of growth, connection, and experience.

I remember asking a million times: how could these people not hate Americans? We function as if they don't exist. We and other "superpowers" reign terror on their little country and many other small places.

They explained that they hate our American government but love our American faces. A large and unchanging country like mine could never fathom that kind of grace and forgiveness.

We spoke with people who were integral parts of the independence of Grenada. It was revolutionary to me to speak with actual revolutionaries—people who refused to accept mistreatment and denial of rights, people who were willing to go to any extent to get their education and stretch their minds in ways that would make a change and landed them in UN meetings, in and out of different governance, and, eventually, an entire People's Revolutionary Government of Grenada.[28]

This government was described to me as a utopia. They were finally seeing the results they had always dreamed of but never received, due to the overbearing colonial powers. Literacy campaigns and plans toward economic prosperity arose, but this dream was short-lived. The closer relations Grenada had to Cuba, the more they were a target.

Soon enough, bombs were sprayed all over their country. I was hearing for the first time what it is like to have your entire country go into a panic with the sounds of grenades clouding your thoughts. I would never have to consider such a reality as an American, being lucky enough to be protected from it in my country of origin.

---

28  "The Grenada Revolution—March 13th, 1979," National Portal of the Government of Grenada, accessed May 9, 2020.

Soon after, the leaders of their government were brutally murdered. Days later, the big great United States swooped in to "save" and invade. The country would never recover from this. Literacy rates began to drop, and political activity became dangerous. Their dreams and hopes of a better, more prosperous country were dismantled in a real way, not in a "divide on free college and the legalization of marijuana" American way.

All of my worries about my country started to look different. It wasn't that they weren't valid but that they had been focused in the wrong direction. They were focused on the issues presented to me but never outside of the same things I saw repeatedly in every article. I needed to be enraged by my government but not because I disagreed with one party more than the other. I needed to be enraged with my government every single time it acted in the imperialist, white supremacist, or callous way that it had since its very foundation. I needed to hold all entities responsible because the way Americans act as if we are the only people on this Earth who matter is disgusting. My American social justice warrior mindset needed serious adjusting.

# Third-Year Cheers

I am now in my third year of college. If I am being honest, I wasn't sure I would ever make it here. Moving away, getting into college, and starting this journey was one thing. But I was never sure I could stay here, survive, and even excel.

In the beginning, I begged my parents to expect the bare minimum of me, that Cs in fact make degrees. That kind of attitude was deeply rooted in the fact that I felt like an imposter in this space. I felt like it was just a miracle that I ended up this far, so it would be inevitable that I struggle through it. But I surprise myself more every day. I adapt to my surroundings in ways I thought I never could and made all As these past semesters. I made everyone proud—friends, family, and my ancestors.

Giving myself permission to be proud of myself is certainly new. A long history of gifted and honors classes intended to make me feel special just taught me to continuously demand more of myself because nothing is ever enough. I never celebrated good grades because it was normal and expected. I never celebrated my success because I was ready to conquer the next expectation.

Thinking of myself in terms of someone else's narration. Thinking like the television and corporate media journalists. Thinking like Hollywood movie writers and characters in Netflix series. Thinking like my teachers and tenured professors. Thinking like a member of an individualistic nation, only considering the collective in the wrong ways, only ever offering views based around the same perspective.

Thinking like everyone else but me.

* * *

Every time I believe I am thinking freely without bias, I run into another scenario where my glasses aren't necessarily rose or any other color. In fact, my glasses are sometimes in any shade that lacks color. I usually wear glasses that were never intended for me and make me feel out of place, as I am looking through the white perspective—the kind of outlook that makes the world look a lot duller.

This third year, I decided to become more involved in an organization with the intent to provide quality of life care for Georgian children infected or affected by HIV/AIDS. Being in this club filled me with inspiration and made me feel like I was doing important work. I focused so much on what it was doing for me that I forgot to analyze what exactly we were doing for others. Like the many other philanthropies and clubs on campus, I worked in ways I secretly criticized. I could point out the white savior complex in every organization but the one I was in. My bias checked me at the door once again.

We prided ourselves on having relationships with the kids we raised money for. But we failed to facilitate impactful conversation when we interacted with these children. I never took the time to notice this. My glasses completely blurred the fact that almost every single member of this organization was white and suburban, and the children were all black and impoverished. While it was important for college students to help and give back, I started to realize some things way after the fact, like that no one in our club even knew how to interact.

I have black friends and black cousins. I often listen to black music, and I have black experiences. So connecting with these kids was never new or out of the ordinary to me. You would think this would bring a white savior agenda to my attention, but I was so busy dancing with them to rap music and talking to them about how I should braid my hair that I never even noticed the actions of those around me. Most of the members had no idea what to even talk to these kids about.

I asked why we didn't talk to these kids about going to college or otherwise try to have a bigger influence on them, but I was told we weren't there to discipline. What were we there for? Smiles and surface-level conversation? In reality, they never interacted with black or impoverished kids in their neighborhoods or private high schools. While they wanted to serve this community, they didn't have all the tools.

I didn't notice until I witnessed the white members of our organization repeatedly assume that one of the new black organization members was one of the kids in our program. They told a very grown black college student to go use the bathroom and asked if she ate lunch. This made it clear to me that no one even knew who these kids really were; they just knew they were all black. I knew what their excuse would be—treating a college student as they treated the other kids, like a charity case, was, of course, an accident not an attack.

After I started paying attention to what was happening, I saw that some members were only there to boost their resumes and leadership skills. But more of them genuinely wanted to help and be the change they wanted to see in the world. And as for the children, I think all they saw was more white people trying to save them rather than aid them, more people providing them pity and charity but, once again, an experience lacking closeness and connection—more people who didn't look like them or talk like them who did a mediocre job of trying to inspire them. While they appreciated the gifts and trips, I think this was just another reminder of the kinds of people who made it in life and to college. Not having anyone remotely like them mentoring them was unarguably symbolic.

* * *

All in all, no matter how many different experiences I have had that made me realize I am black or more in tune with marginalized communities, just as many show me that sometimes... *I am just as out of touch.* There will always be situations where things will go over my head, or my privilege will block me from seeing the different perspectives. That is important, and we must all digest it. Sometimes we will be wrong, biased, unhelpful, or out of touch. But it takes constant vulnerability, self-reflection, humility, and willingness to realize that much.

I will learn forever. I will be checking my biases at the door when I am sixty. Because the world around me moves in ways far greater than my understanding. There are things I don't know, understand, or experience—as a college student, as a biracial person, as an American. But as I live and grow into new spaces and move to new places, my mind and comprehension will grow with me as long as I allow myself to continue to grow, as long as I allow myself to be the living creature that I am... a human—an imperfect, polluting, loving, know-it-all, passionate, over-consuming human.

I must allow myself to be a human who exists in both privilege and oppression, accepting the fact that I don't always know how to discern between the two—not always appreciating the privilege of having access to things and attending a top public university but not also forgetting to acknowledge that my family worked ten times harder than some so I could have these things.

The duality in my life allows me to tap into different perspectives, but I will have to take off my blinding glasses a million more times to really see all the things the world brings.

I feel so eager to encourage others to join me in accepting their privilege and understanding the concept of oppression. But just like me, their eyes will adjust to the world around them at their own pace. They might be lucky enough to only ever see the world in ways that serve them. Or they might run into people like me who, for the first time, make them feel out of place. They might allow themselves to hear my stories or consider my reflections. They just might allow someone to lead their thinking in a different direction.

I will continue to meet people where they are—not in compliant ways but in ways that show I am resilient. But, exhausted from trying to yank and pull them to see what I see, I can only paint them a picture of what life looks like from my glasses—hoping they will also allow me to see their vision, wholeheartedly rejecting the narrative sold to us based solely on our division.

# Conclusion

On my walk today, I made the split-second decision not to kill an ant. It took mental and physical discipline to fight the urge to step on it as it crawled quickly past my foot. I asked myself, "Why did I feel it was necessary to protect the life of an ant?"

But the more important question was why did I want to kill it?

Maybe it was because I am traumatized by the ant bites that covered my feet and ankles as I grew up. Maybe it was because, at some point, I was taught I should be afraid of ants. Maybe it was because this ant looked particularly large and had the kind of speed I wanted to prove to myself I could beat. That ant, and most ants I see, inspire something in me that makes me want to kill them.

But I felt it was necessary to fight the urge and protect the life of an ant, an innocent creature who did no harm to me, just existing in the universe as its creator intended.

I managed to give that ant more thought and compassion than black people are given in the United States.

\* \* \*

As I revised the chapters of this book, I was revisited by anger and heartbreak—the kind that made me want to quit, lay in my sorrow, grieve, and create a temporary home built by my sadness. The world is living in a global pandemic plagued by the coronavirus while simultaneously breaking into protests and riots due to hate crimes and police brutality.

On February 23, 2020, Ahmaud Arbery was jogging down the road. Two white men in the neighborhood saw his black silhouette and concluded that he was a suspect. Without further thought, these men grabbed their guns and chased Ahmaud down the street. After a pursuit that lasted over four minutes, Ahmaud was forced to fight for his life. He lost that fight when one of the men shot two bullets that left him lifeless on the ground.[29]

I was immediately sick when I read this story—another unarmed black man killed for no reason, a tragic event that took place in the city of Brunswick, Georgia, the same one that raised me and inspired my fears.

While writing about my life and the things that made me want to scream, I couldn't figure out why my story was important. Being a person of color in the South gifted me intriguing stories, but I didn't know if it was worth the backlash I would face from my hometown. I was scared they would invalidate my stories or misconstrue my motives.

---

29  Angela Barajas, "Case of Georgia Man Who Was Chased and Killed While Jogging Will Go to Grand Jury," CNN, 2020.

My story is important because of the story of Ahmaud Arbery. We both graduated from Brunswick High School. We grew up with the same teachers in the same rotten buildings.

Even though I wasn't always aware of it, he is the reason I wrote this book. His life deserved to be protected. His murderers should have had the mental and physical discipline to fight the urge that their racist upbringing brought upon them. Instead, they did not have the capacity to value a human life.

Maybe they were taught to act with fear, or maybe they just wanted to prove to themselves that they had the ability to beat him. But they don't even possess the courage to admit it.

I have the courage, the audacity, to call things out for what they are. I am filled with bravery as I expose the uncomfortable truths of my town—the truths that cover the South and fill many American cities, the truths that plague the world.

These truths are simple. Not all of our identities are treated equally. This country is still fueled by the same racism and colonialism that built its patriarchal structure. And in return, our minds are corrupted by the experiences we face in our lifetime.

\* \* \*

I was born into a society and environment that started a battle inside of me—a battle that made me feel like I was less than, like I had to work a lot harder for the same results as everyone else, like no matter what I did, there was no hope.

It began to feel like change was impossible—that all people were mean and hateful, that the world would always hold me back.

These are all lies, yet these lies were my truths for most of my life.

The actual truth was not all identities are treated equally, but my truth was my identity didn't matter. The actual truth was our minds are corrupted by the experiences we face in our lifetime, but my truth was all people are mean and hateful. The actual truth was this country is still fueled by the same racism and colonialism that built its patriarchal structure, but my truth was the world would always hold me back.

The minute differences in those statements were enough to make me want to give up. I wasn't completely aware of the larger structure I was birthed into. I took everything personally without giving myself the time and care to process what was happening.

These lies woke me up in the morning and kept me from sleeping at night. These lies were reinforced by my agonizing interactions at school and assisted by each unpleasant experience I had when I went into the public. These lies broke my heart and attempted to strip away my passion to change the world.

I could point the finger at everyone and everything else but never back at myself. I was angry about everything that ever happened to me. I was bitter because, deep down, I knew I had been compliant to this existing order in so many ways. I allowed it to rule my entire life. I allowed this order to make me overthink who to be friends with, how to do my hair, or the kind of person I should date.

I am now thankful for this anger. I am thankful that this anger turned into resentment and made me want to do something revolutionary. I am thankful that I became so fed up, drained, and exhausted from how I perceived life that I wanted to scream from the rooftops.

That anger fueled the writing of each page in this book. It led me on the most beautiful journey, full of self-reflection and self-assertion. Recalling each memory and thought that stirred something in my soul was the best kind of healing I could have ever come across.

If I am being completely honest, I am terrified for you to read what I have written on these pages. But every fiber in my body wants to share it with the world.

If my words start a revolution in your soul or maybe even a thought you never had before, you should know that the change starts within yourself. It will take a change in each of our souls and minds to create the world we want to see. I have always thought of the quote, "Be the change you want to see in the world" as a call to action for advocates to physically do something. But now, I know it is a lot more than that. Being the change requires a full emotional commitment to rejecting the existing order of society—saying no to the things that don't serve you or those around you, walking the talk both mentally and physically.

The authenticity of our souls will bring justice and peace to our universe. As we reject the assimilation and self-loathing we encounter over our lifetimes, our Power will shine through and work far greater than any tool formed against us.

We the People have the Power. This statement will always reign true; no matter how inaccurate it feels at times.

The Power cannot be found in the language we all share or the spaces we occupy. The Power will never be presented in the language we were taught in school or the talking points we pick up from politicians online. The Power is in the language that is exclusive to our homes and communities. It flows through the music we create that is deemed inappropriate. The dances we break into when we feel like no one is watching. The prayers we pray at night as our ancestors overlook. We share the Power within the stories that some cannot and will not understand. That Power fuels our art and wakes the spirit in our bodies.

This Power is "what works to effect everything which is beyond the ordinary power of men, outside of the common processes of nature; it is present in the atmosphere of life, attaches itself to persons and to things, and is manifested by results which can only be ascribed to its operation."[30]

* * *

As we manifest our Power and fight the injustices we face, we will feel the motions of confrontation.

---

30  R.H. Codrington, "The Melanesians," Oxford: *The Clarendon Press*, 1891, 118-119.

It begins with *we are already dead*. "In the world as it is, we do not count."[31]

This pessimistic attitude almost feels soothing to the soul. You may tell yourself, "What's the point of trying? Nothing will work anyway. Nothing in the world matters. Nothing I do will ever matter." You feel relief in shutting yourself down because, at least that way, less work has to be done.

As we accept that statement, we will realize that *we can be reborn*. "Having accepted the evaluation of what is, agreeing to be the most worthless of things, we can be reborn. We have nothing to hang on to. No old identity to stop us from identifying with a new world... a new world will certainly be born of the fire we shall create. You, the enemy, on the other hand, must cling to what is, must seek to stamp out the flames, and at best can only end sorrowing at a world that cannot remain the same. Eventually, you will be consumed."[32]

So nothing matters. Nothing has any meaning. Therefore, those crippling thoughts don't mean anything either. Since nothing means anything, you might as well allow yourself to dream again, create again, breathe again— betraying your old pessimist self by rediscovering what it feels like to be a human again.

This will make it clear that *we have the stomach for the fight*. "We can strike to kill for the old world is not ours but one in

---

31  Robert L. Scott and Donald K. Smith, "The Rhetoric of Confrontation," *Quarterly Journal of Speech* 55, no. 1 (1969): 6.

32  Ibid.

which we are already dead, in which killing injures us not, but provides us with the chance of rebirth."[33]

After existing in a world where you were already dead, what else is there to lose? Your past is painted by trauma, and you know the feeling of pain all too well. So you decide you have nothing left to be afraid of. You can finally see the scars all over you. You are no longer brainwashing yourself in favor of your abuser. Therefore, no one can hurt you anymore.

This will finally grant us the feeling we deserve; *we are united and understand.* "We have accepted our past as past by willing our future. Since you must cling to the past, you have no future and cannot even understand."[34]

The picture is bigger now. In the past, you could only see the part where things were dark. But the picture began to reveal the rest of itself against your will. The light was so bright to the point that it was almost disturbing to the eye. But now you can finally see, and everything looks so much clearer. You begin to notice the empty parts of the picture that hold space for you to create while the people around you are still stuck in one place.

*To Hear a Girl Scream* is a memoir of my life that presents my transitions from *we are already dead* to *we can be reborn* to *we have the stomach for the fight* to *we are united and understand.*

This was the book where I finally got to scream. After feeling like I was being silenced all my life, I got to scream to the

---

33  Ibid.

34  Ibid.

point where I lost my voice. It was debilitating to relive the most heartbreaking and confusing moments of my life. But then I was granted the sweet solitude that allowed me to hear myself. To understand myself. To feel myself. So now, I will consciously choose to hear myself instead of others— focusing on my own thoughts, reflections, and desires, finally using my mind instead of my mouth to drown out the white noise.

All this time, I thought all I wanted was to scream. But I just needed to scream so I could hear myself dream.

# Appendix

**PART 1**

**THE YEAR 1999**

History.com Editors. "Columbine Shooting." HISTORY, 2009. Accessed April 14, 2020. https://www.history.com/topics/1990s/columbine-high-school-shootings.

History.com Editors. "Teen Gunman Kills 17, Injures 17 At Parkland, Florida High School." HISTORY, 2019. Accessed April 14, 2020. https://www.history.com/this-day-in-history/parkland-marjory-stoneman-douglas-school-shooting.

History.com Editors. "Sandy Hook School Shooting." HISTORY, 2013. Accessed April 14, 2020. https://www.history.com/this-day-in-history/gunman-kills-students-and-adults-at-newtown-connecticut-elementary-school.

"What Happened In 1999 Inc. Pop Culture, Prices, and Events." Thepeoplehistory.com. Accessed April 14, 2020. http://www.thepeoplehistory.com/1999.html.

### GENERATION ZOOMER

Tetrault, Sam. "What Is a Zoomer (Gen Z) & Who's Considered One?" Cake Blog, 2020. Accessed April 17, 2020. https://www.joincake.com/blog/zoomer/.

Wang, Hansi Lo. "Generation Z Is the Most Racially and Ethnically Diverse Yet." NPR, 2018. Accessed April 17, 2020. https://www.npr.org/2018/11/15/668106376/generation-z-is-the-most-racially-and-ethnically-diverse-yet.

## PART 2

### MIXED WITH TWO

"Loving V. Virginia." *Oyez*. Accessed April 25, 2020. https://www.oyez.org/cases/1966/395.

### TOKEN BLACK FRIENDS

Curtis, Christopher Paul. *Bud, Not Buddy*. Delacorte Books for Adult Readers, 1999.

Epstein, Rebecca, Jamilia Blake, and Thalia González. "Girlhood Interrupted: The Erasure of Black Girls' Childhood." *SSRN Electronic Journal*, 2017. https://www.law.georgetown.edu/poverty-inequality-center/wp-content/uploads/sites/14/2017/08/girlhood-interrupted.pdf.

## PART 3

### MIDDLE SCHOOL DROOLS

Meier, Kenneth J. "Teachers, Students, and Discrimination: The Policy Impact of Black Representation." *The Journal of Politics* 46, no. 1 (1984): 261-262. doi:10.2307/2130443.

Patchin, Justin W., and Sameer Hinduja. "Cyberbullying and Self-Esteem." *Journal of School Health* 80, no. 12 (2010): 614. doi:10.1111/j.1746-1561.2010.00548.x.

### HIGH SCHOOL FOOLS

"Brunswick High School Student Body." U.S. News & World Report. Accessed May 8, 2020. https://www.usnews.com/education/best-high-schools/georgia/districts/glynn-county/brunswick-high-school-5929/student-body.

### SENIORITIS

Drutman, Lee. "America Is Now the Divided Republic the Framers Feared." *The Atlantic*, 2020. Accessed May 8, 2020. https://www.theatlantic.com/ideas/archive/2020/01/two-party-system-broke-constitution/604213/.

## PART 4

### FIRST-YEAR TEARS

Moore, Mary T. "UGA Fact Book 2018, 50th Edition." Oir.Uga.Edu, 2018. https://oir.uga.edu/_resources/files/factbook/UGA_FactBook2018.pdf.

**SECOND-YEAR FEARS**

"Brian Kemp: 'So Conservative'—Campaign 2018." Video. *The Washington Post*, 2018. Accessed May 9, 2020. https://www. washingtonpost.com/video/politics/other/brian-kemp-so-conservative—campaign-2018/2018/07/25/46743c34-903c-11e8-ae59-01880eac5f1d_video.html.

Friedman, Zack. "78% of Workers Live Paycheck to Paycheck." *Forbes*, 2019. Accessed May 9, 2020. https://www.forbes.com/ sites/zackfriedman/2019/01/11/live-paycheck-to-paycheck-government-shutdown/#648807004f10.

Haltiwanger, John. "Georgia Voters Face Long Lines, Malfunctioning Voter Machines Amid Hotly Contested Governor's Race." *Business Insider*, 2018. Accessed May 9, 2020. https:// www.businessinsider.com/georgia-governor-brian-kemp-stacey-abrams-long-lines-malfunctioning-voter-machines-midterms-2018-11.

Knowles, Hannah, and Reis Thebault. "Georgia Purged 309,000 Voters from Its Rolls. It's the Second State to Make Cuts in Less Than a Week." *The Washington Post*, 2019. Accessed May 9, 2020. https://www.washingtonpost.com/nation/2019/12/17/ georgia-purged-voters-its-rolls-its-second-state-make-cuts-less-than-week/.

"Meet Stacey | Stacey Abrams For Governor." Join Stacey Abrams, 2018. Accessed May 9, 2020. https://staceyabrams.com/ meet-stacey/.

Shah, Khushbu. "'Textbook Voter Suppression': Georgia's Bitter Election A Battle Years in the Making." *The Guardian*, 2018.

https://www.theguardian.com/us-news/2018/nov/10/georgia-election-recount-stacey-abrams-brian-kemp.

"The Grenada Revolution—March 13, 1979." National Portal of the Government of Grenada. Accessed May 9, 2020. https://www.gov.gd/grenada-revolution.

## CONCLUSION

Barajas, Angela. "Case of Georgia Man Who Was Chased and Killed While Jogging Will Go to Grand Jury." CNN, 2020. https://www.cnn.com/2020/05/05/us/ahmaud-arbery-jogging-georgia-shooting/index.html.

Codrington, R.H. "The Melanesians." Oxford: *The Clarendon Press*, 1891. 118-119.

Scott, Robert L. and Donald K. Smith. "The Rhetoric of Confrontation." *Quarterly Journal of Speech* 55, no. 1 (1969): 6. https://doi.org/10.1080/00335636909382922.

# Acknowledgments

First, I want to thank my family for loving, supporting, and, most importantly, having faith in me. Mom, Dad, and Chris, thank you for believing in me more than I believed in myself at times. You guys have always seen the magic inside of me and have helped me see it too.

Thank you to those who listened to me rant for countless hours and have been there for me to lean on. Thank you to my friends who read my work and provided heartwarming feedback that made me want to continue pushing forward. To my best friends, Charis, Kamryn, and Christian, thank you for always accepting me, giving me space to unapologetically be myself, and being open to learning from me. Madds, thank you for opening my heart and redefining what family means to me.

A special thank you to Cariel Rozier for being my partner in crime and sister since the fourth grade. Any problem you have, I also have.

Thank you to everyone who allowed me to interview you and pick your minds over this writing process. I appreciate your willingness to answer my complicated questions and share new perspectives with me. Many of these stories were inspired by our conversations.

Thank you to the creators of the anthology *This Bridge Called My Back*, Cherríe Moraga and Gloria Anzaldúa, for being a constant inspiration and providing me with relatable stories when I needed them most. By giving radical women of color a voice, you have left the most beautiful of marks on this world for the rest of eternity.

Thank you to New Degree Press, Eric Koester, and Brian Bies for giving me the opportunity to share my story. A special thank you to my editor, Emily Price, for providing constant encouragement, helping me convey my message, and also being a friend.

Lastly, thank you to my Beta readers and those who preordered or donated to my book campaign. This book came to life because of you:

Abby S., Adiah B., Akaylie F., Altamese R., Amanda F., Amy B., Andrew P., Angela N., Angelo S., Anna G., Ashley K., Ashley S., Avalon K., Baeisha H., Bailey M., Berrien G., Blayne M., Blondine J., Brandon F., Cariel R., Carol B., Caroline M., Celeste S., Charis W., Chase H., Cheri B., Christian N., Christopher C., Cindy K., Cory M., Curtiesha H., Daniela C., Darrin R., David H., Dawn K., Dee W., Dee H., Demere H., Derek M., Destiny W., Destiny D., Elaina M., Elizabeth T., Elizabeth R., Elle D., Emma B., Eric K., Erica L., Garrison H., Gavin B., Grant A., Haleigh A., Harmoni C., Hayley C., Imir R., Jade A., Jaidyn S., Jamie W., Jan W., Jane M., Jazmin N.,

Jennifer S., John W., Jordan W., Jordan B., Julia W., June L., Kaitlin F., Kamryn H., Katherine D., Kathryn B., Kathryn and Larry C., Katissa M., Katrina G., Kelly D., Keenan W., Kevin W., Latasha R., Lauren C., LeAndra C., LeiLani C., Linzi S., Liz A., Lula W., Mackenzie S., Mamie K., Marisa L., Marshall T., Mary Margaret C., Meika B., Michael B., Mikayla W., Miranda O., Morgan S., Morgan M., Nancy V., Nia P., Noelle M., Peyton R., Rebekah W., Robert M., Ronie S., Sarah C., Savanna H., Serkan C., Shannon B., Shannon S., Sherry M., Susan C., Sydney B., Teeg S., Tiffany L., Tommy M., Tonya P., Torrence B., Trey C., Wesley O., Willie D., Willie H., and Zella O.

Made in the USA
Columbia, SC
13 August 2020